CAROLYN WRIGHT

DEATH
OF A SPOUSE

*A Memoir of Loving
through Lung Cancer*

Sh'Shares NETWORK

DEATH OF A SPOUSE:
A Memoir of Loving Through Lung Cancer

Copyright © 2017 by Carolyn Wright

All rights reserved. No portion of this publication may be reproduced, distributed, or transmitted in any form or by any means, including photocopying, recording, or other electronic or mechanical methods, without the prior written permission of the publisher, except in the case of brief quotations embodied in critical reviews and certain other noncommercial uses permitted by copyright law.

For permission requests, write to the publisher, addressed
"ATTN: Permissions" at the following:

Sh'Shares NETWORK, LLC
1601-1 N Main Street 13202
Jacksonville, FL 32206-0202
www.ShShares.com

Bulk discounts are available on quantity purchases by associations, corporations, and others for business, educational and ministry use. For details, contact the publisher at the address above.

Library of Congress Control Number: 2017964081

ISBN: 978-1-942650-73-7 (print)
        978-1-942650-74-4 (eBook)

Printed in the United States of America

Contents

Introduction 5
Late January 1993 9
February 1993 11
    February 13 11
    February 20 11
    February 21 12
    February 22 12
    February 23 12
    February 24 12
March 1993 15
    March 11 15
April 1993 17
    April 26 17
    April 27 17
    April 28 17
    April 29 18
    April 30 19
May 1993 21
    May 1 21
    May 2 21
    May 3 22
    May 4 22
    May 5 23
    May 6 26
    May 7 27
    May 8 29
    May 9 29
    May 10 31
    May 11 35
    May 12 39
    May 13 42
    May 14 44
    May 15 46
    May 16 49
    May 17 52
    May 18 54
    May 19 55
    May 20 57
    May 21 59

May 22	60
May 23	60
May 24	61
May 25	62
May 30	62

June 1993 65

June 1	65
June 2	65
June 4	66
June 5	66
June 6	67
June 7	68
June 8	68
June 9	70
June 10	72
June 11	74
June 12	77
June 13	80
June 14	81
June 15	83
June 16	85
June 17	86
June 18	87
June 19	89
June 20	91
June 21	93
June 22	95
June 23	98
June 24	101
June 25	102
June 26	104
June 27	105
June 28	107

July 1993 111

July 2	111
July 3	112
July 4	112
July 6	114

Introduction

When I look back, I can see that some things changed.

The children and I started going to church all the time. We enjoyed the saved life. We would go out to dinner on Friday nights before we got saved.

That changed. Now that the children and I were in church, my husband did not want to follow us. Despite that, everything seemed to be okay. I still wanted him to be saved, yet he would not listen to anything I had to say.

He always knew it all.

Things just had to be his way.

> Husbands listen to your wife.
> Wives listen to your husband.
> ***Always have good communication.***
> It is always good to ask,
> "Did you mean to say...?"
> Make sure you know what he or she is saying.
> Say what you mean and mean what you say.

One day, I saw something that looked like a rising in his armpit. I told him to tell the doctor about it because when I was in nursing school, I learned that was one of the signs of cancer.

He said, "I am not going to tell him anything. He will find it."

Years passed.

There was an old lady that came from my hometown, Valdosta, GA. She lived with my mama and my sister. When mama died, she came to Florida to live with us.

I thought it was okay with him. I later found out he didn't like it. He kept telling me I needed to get a job. He was well able to take care of the household. He had a very good job. He also had rental property. He did not want me to know how to handle that part of the business. I would try to talk to him about the apartments and the houses. He would talk so ugly to me about it.

One night, I wanted to buy something for the house, so I went to the house where he was working. I felt so good. I had been praying and I had a spiritual high. I walked in the house and asked for some money. He talked so ugly and threw a broom at me. I was so hurt. I left there crying.

This was the beginning of his transition. I later found out another woman was there, and he had to get me away. Before that, he had never been violent with me. He did say I need to get a job.

Later, I wrote this letter to him:

3/26/90

Otis,

I am truly sorry that (after almost 28 years of marriage) you say you are sick of me. I guess I have been living in a fantasy world thinking you love me as much as I love you.

I am sorry I have not been the wife you wanted me to be. I hope and pray your next wife will do better than I have done.

It seems we have come to the end. It doesn't make sense for me to keep making you miserable and sick. You see, I feel that I am doing what the Lord will have me to do, that is taking care of Miss Sister. I love you, but I will not go against what the Lord will have me to do to please you.

Do you think it is easy to listen to you put me down about working when I know I can get a job and do for myself and my daughter? Well, it is not easy, but my God has all power in His hand, more power than you or me, and I will not go against Him. I don't know long I will have to take care of her, but so long as the Lord says to, I am going to do it. I don't want to defy you, but I'd rather defy you than God because He has the power of life and death.

I have called my job for another case and they don't have any work right now. That is the only job I intend to have right now. If this doesn't sit well with you, I advise you to pray and talk to God. After you do that, if you want a divorce, I will not try to stop you. And if you think I want everything you've got, forget it. When we got married, we didn't have anything, and the way it is in my life, I still don't have anything so don't worry about what you have to give me. It really doesn't matter. I know God will take care of me.

If we are to stay together, we have to come together as one. You can't keep the business secret from me. God is not pleased.

When I get back, we can talk if you want to. If not, then I'll know it is over.

Think about this too: If you should lose everything now, can you handle that? I can because I don't have any material things, but I do have the Lord.

And if the Lord is telling me what to do, and you are fighting against me, then you are fighting against the Lord.

Think too about what happens every time you come against me. I don't want to be hurt, so let's get it together or we will part.

Your Choice
Kay

I don't know if he read the letter or not.

Well, we stayed together. We had some good times in our marriage. We went on cruises. We enjoyed each other. We also went on trips with some of his co-workers. We traveled to Canada and to New Orleans. Those were some of the good times. There were times on some of those trips when he would act ugly to me. I would always forgive him.

Otis never thought he did anything wrong. There came a time when he got distant from me. I could not do anything to please him.

I loved him, but I loved God more. I was very involved in church. Our children were involved too. He was active in his church also. I would pray for him. I found a prayer that I wrote to God asking for his healing. At that time, I did not know Otis was sick. I would always pray for him no matter how he treated me. I wanted us to stay together. I wanted him to get saved so we could serve the Lord together.

> Husbands and wives, learn how to love and treasure one another.
>
> ***Pray for each other.***
>
> You don't know how important your prayers for each other are.

I didn't listen.

...not until I wanted God to do something for me.

My husband was all for my praying for him until he found out it was related to him going to church. That was when he told me he was doing something for this young lady at another church. His church. It was the same woman I was already suspicious of.

Late January 1993

Here we are now. Late January is when it starts.

It is very cold outside. Almost as cold as it is in my home.

I went to the front door one day and opened it. I put my head out and told God, "I have had enough! Do what you want!" Little did I know what was about to happen in my life. I couldn't go back and tell God I didn't mean it like that.

I tried to take it back.

I tried with my husband. I did.

I tried to make our marriage better.

I tried praying for him... hoping it would get better. It didn't last. He went back to be his same ole nasty self to me.

You will see later what I am talking about.

February 1993

February 13

In February, around the 13th, my husband Otis started to cough really bad. Then, he started to have the blackouts. He would only be out for a little while. When he came back to consciousness, he would say, "I was just teasing."

I took him to the doctor.

The doctor ordered x-rays, but he never called us back.

February 20

On February 20, I had a conversation with the Lord.

I was praying for Otis' salvation. I was getting uneasy about what was going on. I called my pastor. He prayed for me and Otis.

Otis had me to call Tony to come and bring him a peach soda. Margaret came by with a soda too. His sister Bay called to check on him.

Tony came to visit. I was in the kitchen cooking Sunday dinner waiting for the family to come over. After leaving our house that day, Tony called to check on things. I told him I was calling the cardiac doctor.

The doctor told me to take Otis to the emergency room, but Otis did not want to go. Tony had to come back and talk to him. He got him in the car and took him to the hospital. As we sat in the waiting room, Dr. Lesene came out to speak with me. He stated that Otis had fluid around the heart. He cupped his hands to demonstrate.

February 21

It is now February 21.

I called Trey to call Pastor and Pop. I was pacing the floor.

Otis was admitted to room 321. Later, Dr. Dean came out to talk with Trey, Tony and me in the waiting room. *Dr. Dean is one of the leading heart specialists in the city.* We were allowed to visit with Otis. We prayed. He was looking better, yet we were told we could not stay with him, so we left.

February 22

On February 22, Dr. Stilt performed surgery. He sent the fluid to pathology.

Otis was not breathing properly, so they intubated[1] him.

He was so afraid.

February 23

- ~ Next day.
- ~ Results came back from pathology. No cancer was found in the fluid.

His coworkers came. They were very saddened.

Tiny, our goddaughter, came to visit too.

We put in a call to Tricey. She came home from being away at college.

February 24

Dr. Kawaaf came in on February 24.

This doctor said that cancer was in the fluid.

He turned Otis' care over to Dr. Luke, a cancer specialist. Dr. Luke ordered a body scan and a bronchoscopy[2]. Dr. Dean ordered an

---

[1] When a tube is placed into a person's airways to keep them open and to administer drugs or to attach to a ventilator to assist with breathing

[2] A test done to visualize a patient's airways

echocardiogram[3].

The family was upset and crying.

There were tests done... biopsies[4] of the lymph nodes[5]. Definite cancer cells were found.

He has squamous cell cancer[6]. The lung is the origin.

I thought back to the times that I told him to see a doctor about those risings under his armpit and he wouldn't do it. He was bull-headed. He did not listen to anything I said. He always had to be right and do everything his way.

Church members came to visit. Ministers Jones and Fields came from our church, Philippian Community Church. Reverend Calhoun came from the church Otis went to, New Bethlehem Baptist Church.

After the biopsy was done, Otis had chemotherapy on March 8th, 9th, and 10th.

~ He had nausea and was vomiting.

---

[3] A test done to take images of a patient's heart

[4] A tissue sample taken to from the body to be examined when initial tests are abnormal

[5] Small glands in the body that carry fluids, wastes, and nutrients

[6] A form of cancer that develops in skin cells

> Husbands treat your wives with respect.
> Wives treat your husbands with respect.
>
> ***Love and care for each other.***
>
> We don't know when death will come.

March 1993

March 11

- ~ He was discharged.
- ~ He had no appetite.
- ~ He was still nauseous, vomiting and coughing.
- ~ Medication was $197.00.
- ~ His temperature was elevated at times.
- ~ We gave him Tylenol.

Also in March...

- ~ Doctor visit.
- ~ Vital signs okay. He went to the lab.
- ~ Complete blood count doing good.
- ~ 4/5 chemo treatment in doctor's office.

- ~ 1st day fine. Eating.
- ~ 2nd day okay. Eating. Weaker.
- ~ 3rd day. Tired. Feeling weaker.
- ~ Otis is still losing weight and this temperature is still high at 102°.

Dr. Sharpe was consulted for medication for Otis' voice. He was given antibiotics. During the next visit, he was given Ensure.

Dr. Luke called. Dr. Kawaaf returned our call. He wanted Otis to go to Methodist ER. The nurses and doctors remember him from before. I.V. antibiotics given. Cat scan was done. As we waited for results, we went to Dr. Luke's and to the lab for a complete blood count[7] exam. It was good. Dr. Luke says scan show no increase in growth of the tumor. There was some fluid still around the heart. He doesn't hold out much hope for Otis. Referred him to Dr. Schoopel for radiation therapy.

---

[7] A measurement of various elements of blood, aids in diagnosis and treatment of conditions and diseases.

April 1993

April 26

~ Doctor Schoopel explained x-rays

From beginning to this point, she saw a difference in the x-rays. The tissue looked better. She says there is a fifty-fifty chance of shrinking the tumor.
Otis was taken to the back and mark for radiation. There were blue marks on chin near his neck and all over the chest, like a window.

April 27

~ First radiation.

Everything is fine. We went straight home.
He was tired and sleepy. He slept most of the afternoon.
He ate a sandwich from Blue boys.

April 28

~ 2nd day of radiation. Treatment fast. Felt tired.

We needed work done on the car. He was insistent about going right now.
As we were sitting there, he got up and went outside. I watched from the window. I could see him throwing up.
It was a long day. I asked him if he wanted something to drink. He

wanted apple juice. He said there wasn't any place close by. I looked up and saw a Lil Champs. I told him I will walk down there. He said it is too far. I took off walking. It only took five minutes to get there. I purchased a sandwich for me and apple juice for both of us. I left the store. As I crossed the street, I thought about crackers. I went back to the store, got the crackers and walked back. It only took fifteen minutes total, there and back. I told him I thought about the crackers and went back to the store. He said, "I was talking to you." I told him about the scripture that says, "If your ways please God, He will answer your prayer before you can ask."

He ate and said he felt better.

Earlier, while he was standing outside the building, Bishop Simmons came up. I was praying that he would see him and pray for him. Otis saw him too and walked over to where he was and spoke to him. Bishop Simmons did not recognize him. Maybe because he had lost so much weight.

After we were home, he drank an Ensure. He was still nauseated.
He went to sleep. When he woke up, he was still nauseated and vomiting. I placed a towel with ice around his neck. That helped stop the nausea.
His appetite was gone. I went to the store to get some soup. He was able to eat the soup and keep it down.

All this time, I have been praying for his healing because I know God can do it.

April 29

~ 3rd day of radiation

We were late. Traffic was backed up. They were waiting for him.
He is still tired and weak from yesterday. He ate very little at breakfast.
He is staying in the back a long time. I hope they have the right Mr. Wright. There are two of them, a black one and a white one.
He has been back there for a long time, an hour or more. It doesn't

usually take this long.

I really need to go to the bathroom. But I think he might come out while I'm gone.

I did go to the bathroom. Boy, do I feel better. He is not back yet. I think I'll go back there to see what's going on.

I walked in the back and was standing at the desk to ask for him when I saw him coming through a door saying, "You looking for me?" Then he told me, he saw the doctor today and that's why it took so long.

We left and went to the Sears Warehouse liquidation sale looking for Boo. We were going to pick up an edger. I let him off at the door and looked for a parking place. It was really crowded. He saw Pat W. and Judy W. and was talking to them when I came back.

We walked into the store looking for the edger and asking questions. No one could help us. I called Gloria to get Boo's phone number. I called him, and he told us who to ask for. No one knew John Daniels.

Otis sat down on a sofa in the store while we looked. I could tell he was tired and not feeling well. I told him to come on. Let's go home.

He waited outside while I got the car. On my way back, I could see him vomiting. I saw one couple asking if they could do anything for him. He told them his wife was right there.

He got in the car and we stopped to get crackers and apple juice. As soon as we got home, he laid in the bed and went to sleep.

He looks so frail. His hair is thinning.

April 30

~ Day four of radiation.

Today, I am prepared. I have the apple juice on ice, peanut butter crackers, and a bag just in case he starts to vomit while we are riding. I have the ice in a towel to help with his nausea.

Treatment was fast. He was in and out before I could relax and talk to the people in the waiting room. However, I did get a chance to talk with Archie, who had come to bring his niece. Four years old with a brain tumor. I had a talk with her mom yesterday and was looking forward to talking to her today about the Lord. I gave her brother one of the church's cards and wrote on the back the times our T.V. ministry comes on.

We left the cancer center and went to Sears Warehouse again. This time before going in, I had him to eat some crackers and drink juice. This seemed to do well.

I dropped him close to the building and parked the car. Boo saw me walking and came over. We went inside and found John Daniels and the edger, and we went to pay for it. The lines were long. We had Otis to go outside and sit down while we waited. After I paid for the edger, I took it to the car and came back to get Otis.

At home, he laid down and went to sleep. Mucus built up and he got up to cough and started to vomit. The cold gets caught in his throat and causes him to gag, so he laid down saying he is tired.

Later that day, I went out to eat with Mae and Miss Sister. Otis did not feel up to going anywhere.

His appetite is very poor. He drinks Ensure Plus sometimes.

Today is our daughter Tricey's birthday. She will be in tomorrow from FSU in Tallahassee, FL. He wants me to get cake and ice cream for her and invite some of her friends and our family over to celebrate.

May 1993

May 1

Every morning, I take his vital signs. Sometimes, before I can take them, he has to cough and get mucus from his throat and lungs.

It is hard watching him lose weight and not eating.

Today was a fair day. Tricey came home. The family came over. We had spaghetti with sausage and shrimp, ice cream, and cake.

Otis ate a little spaghetti and a little ice cream and cake. Thank God, he kept it down.

Later that night...
- ~ Skin is warm.
- ~ Temperature 100.2.
- ~ Tylenol was given. He slept.
- ~ Temperature down when taken later.

His breathing is short. He won't do the incentive spirometer unless I am on him about it. Mucus is building in the lungs.

I watched him as he slept. He slept well. He is still weak.

May 2

This is Sunday morning. He still has no appetite. He tried to get me to go to church. I stay home to watch him. Tricey didn't go because we were having tent service. Otis stayed in bed. I tried to encourage him to get up before people start coming from church.

Leroy, one of his coworkers and his son came by to bring a tape from their church service. They had to wait until he sponged off and dressed. Later, Tricey brought his mom, Mattie Varnadore over to see him. He came up front to sit with her. He asked me to bring him some beans and wieners. I had bought a small can. He ate half of it.

May 3

- ~ Day 5 of radiation therapy.
- ~ His vital signs were good.
- ~ Mucus is building up.
- ~ Coughing and vomiting.

Therapy was over fast again. No chance to read or watch T.V. in the waiting room.

Back home, he ate crackers and cheese, and drink apple juice.

Kailyn, our granddaughter is here, and she is helping him eat the crackers. She would go in the room to see granddaddy and come back with a cracker. I go in to encourage him to use the incentive spirometer. He is tired, but he gets up to do it anyway. I told him the other day that while he was in the hospital he did it all the time. He said they came around every hour to do it. I asked, "Why won't you do for me?" He said that I am not as tough as they were and that he did what they wanted so they'll let him come home. I told him if he didn't do it for me, I was going to put him out.

This evening he had me fix a little plate of food and when I got there with the food, he got up, started coughing and vomiting. I carried the food back to the kitchen because he didn't want it. The inhalers and nasal sprays that he must use before each meal must have triggered something in the throat.

He laid down to rest.

Later, he drank an Ensure Plus.

May 4

- ~ Day 6 of radiation.

This is a day of double duty. Miss Sister has an appointment at 9 am at the Faculty Clinic, and Otis has an appointment at the cancer center at 10 am for his radiation therapy. Thank God Tricey is home. She carried Otis and I carried Miss Sister.

They have just completed a rectal exam on her. Again, the stool has some occult blood in it. They are talking about doing a proctoscope on her. We are just sitting in here waiting for them to come back to tell us something, and I am wondering how Otis is doing. They are supposed to do new markings on him today, narrowing down the field.

The Lord has blessed our finances since Otis has been sick. He has blessed him spiritually and me also. Yesterday I felt down and discouraged. I felt like giving up because Otis didn't want to cooperate. Deborah Hankerson and Mazella talked to me and told me I couldn't give up. I have to stay strong for him. He told me last night that he wanted to stop his medication. This morning, I asked him what he wanted to do. He said he didn't know. I left to come out here with Miss Sister, so I don't know if he took his medication or not.

It is 11 am and we have been sitting in here for about an hour. The doctor finally came in. They have decided to do more tests on her before they do a sigmoidoscope. They want to draw blood today and schedule her to come for an upper GI series and a barium enema, which will be less strenuous for her.

Otis and I had prayer together the other night and the Lord really blessed. Sometimes, when I look at Otis I feel as though the Lord is healing him even though it doesn't look like it. The coughing and vomiting of mucus I feel are clearing his lungs, and that is a healing process.

Later, he is still weak and nauseated.

~ Not eating.

May 5

Today is a very busy day. Otis has three appointments. We are to be at the cancer center at 8:30 am for his radiation. We are running late.

 Angie Bailey went into labor at about 4 am. Bob called for me to meet them at Baptist Hospital to get Reggie. I am tired because I went to bed late. I got to the hospital before they arrived. They came up shortly after I arrived. I got Reggie and came home. Angie looked calm.

 Once at home, I told Reggie to go to sleep on the sofa in the den. He did not want to get in the bed in any of the rooms.

 At about 5:30 am, I got back in bed. I could not go to sleep. As soon as I started to drift off, the doorbell rang. It was Kailyn coming. Lil Trey came in too. Reggie heard his voice and woke up. Trey left for school. I turned the TV on for Reggie and gave Kailyn to Tricey. I got myself ready, took Otis' vital signs, and fixed him something to eat.

 We arrived at the center a few minutes late. They did his treatment quickly and he came out. He was so tired he had to sit in the chair for a moment in the lobby to get his breath. We left and went home. He relaxed a few minutes before we had to go to an office visit with Dr. Luke at 10:30 am.

 At Dr. Luke's, they weighed him. He had lost a pound. Dr. Luke seemed nicer today. He told us the scan showed the tumor was shrinking. That is the first encouragement we have gotten from him.

 We stopped at the lab for blood work. The blood work turned out okay. The white count was fine. We left the office and I had him to sit on a bench outside the building until I got the car.

 On my way back, I could see him vomiting. He had not eaten that much. He says the mucus makes him vomit. As I pulled around the circle, the security guard asked if I would pull the car up out of the way of a truck coming through. I asked him to get me a cup of ice for Otis. I got a towel out of the trunk of the car and put the ice in it to put on his throat. This somehow soothes and calms nausea.

 We got home, and he laid down and went to sleep.

 At Dr. Luke's office, Gladys gave us Ensure Plus. That was a blessing. It cost a lot in the store.

 Otis' appointment with Dr. Sharpe is at 2 pm. We get home about 1:45. He is still tired. Reggie was with us. Tricey had gone shopping and took Kailyn with her.

Dr. Sharpe says he had gained a half pound according to what he weighed the last time. She wanted us to continue the breathing treatments. His temp was up slightly, and she placed him on antibiotics. She gave Reggie some nice little books. Also, she gave us something called Pulmocare[8] instead of Ensure. She said it was good too. She also told us that each radiation treatment was like a surgery. It takes a lot out of you. She advises he gets plenty of rest. What she said helped me a lot because I had been trying to get him to get up when indeed he needed to rest.

At home, he got in the bed and went to sleep.

Cynthia came to get Kailyn. Tricey was not back. She had called to tell me to tell Cyn she will bring Kailyn home. Trey and Reggie started playing, so Cynthia left him for a while to be with Reggie.

Angie had the baby at 11 am this morning, Jeremy William Bailey. Reggie talked to his dad briefly on the phone.

I told Trey and Reggie I was going to take them to McDonald's. They were excited. Reggie is a picky eater.

Deborah came by with DeAndrea and Adrienna. Trey and Reggie didn't want to play with them. I told them they should tell the girls they are sorry, and Reggie said it immediately. Trey said it slowly, low. I asked him what he said. He replied what he said. I told him he would have to say it to the girls his self and he did. Then Trey told the girls, Grandma is going to take us to McDonald and you can't go. Then, I decided to take all of them. Deborah went home and left me with them. I called Mazella and she met us up there. The kids ate and rode on the little ride, like a merry-go-round. Adrienna didn't want to get off.

We left and dropped A and D at their house. I called Otis to see if he needed anything. I carried Trey home. Tricey was there with Kailyn. I played with Kailyn a little while and went home.

I gave Reggie his bath and he wanted to look at basketball on TV. I told him to stay in the room with Otis. He said he wants to look at

---

[8] A diet-management drink and/or food supplement that reduces carbon dioxide production for people with lung diseases

it his room (den). I asked him to stay back there and look at it with granddaddy because I wanted to look at something else and he did. Tricey had washed her hair and was in the den looking at the game too. I wanted to look at the tape of the soap opera. The game was over Reggie came in the den to lay down. I looked at the tape briefly.

I was tired and sleepy. I went to the bathroom and did my Bible reading and prayer. I went to bed.

May 6

Otis is very weak and tired.

We got to the cancer center late, as usual. They carried him back and did the treatment. Bob met me to get Reggie. He talks about the young girl that was at the house last night, Reasey, Gloria Groome's daughter. They came by to see Otis. They were very encouraging. I left Bob and Reggie talking to Brother Howard, who works at the center. I got in the building just as Otis was coming out. We left.

As we were driving home I asked him if he wanted to go to the prayer tower. He asked if anyone was there. I told him yes. He said okay. We got there, and he walked to the door and was tired. I knew he couldn't make it around the walk of faith. I didn't want him to go up there anyway. I knew he was too weak. Someone said the stairs are better, but I told them that was too much too. Deborah got Robert. Robert sent for Louis.

We were in the office and about to start praying when Pastor Callahan came in. He talked (preached) faith, then prayed. The anointing was high. I feel the healing process (the miracle taking place). Otis was praising the Lord. He looked like a different man. God really blessed him. The pastor gave him a bottle of blessed oil too, for a point of contact. In the car, Minister Jones came by and talked to him while I talked to Kirk.

Back home, he went straight to bed. He was weak and tired. I am thinking, "How do I encourage him to accept his healing?" Even though he's tired, I tell him he has to keep praising and thanking God and telling his body that he is healed.

He wanted some fruit, so I went to the store to get watermelon, cantaloupe, and grapes. He ate a little cantaloupe and grapes. Later, he ate watermelon.

Pop came by. We went out east to get an apartment ready. The tenant wanted to move in tomorrow. The refrigerator was not plugged up and it was full of maggots. The stove was awful. It was full of grease. Zina met me over to help clean up. Thank God for her.

I ended up leaving keys with her because I wanted to get home to see our TV ministry. It was a blessing too. Otis watched it with me. He ate a little soup. Then, he went to bed after watching basketball. We had prayer before he ate. Trey came by and he prayed with Otis also.

I tried to watch the tapes of the soaps again. I was tired and falling asleep. I went in my bathroom and read the bible and prayed. I thanked God for saving Otis. I thanked Him for things being as well as they are. I feel in my spirit that he is going to get well.

May 7

Up early to get Tricey up. She has a meeting at one of the schools to observe in the classroom. Beverly Brown set it up for her. While she was getting ready, Adrienne from the office at FSU where Tricey worked, called to tell her she will not be working this summer. I heard her crying. I waited until she came out of the bathroom. She was dressing when I asked what was going on. When she told me, I told her not to worry about it. Everything is going to be all right. She left for her appointment.

I got Otis up for his vital signs. They were okay. He is still tired and weak. He only ate a small amount of grits and spam (something he wants). We left home about 9:45 am. Thinking we are late, I put him off at the door while I find a place to park. I was surprised to see him sitting in the waiting area when I came in. He is usually gone. We were sitting when I heard Maury's talk show come on. I asked him what time was his appointment and he said 10:45. That's when I realized we were almost an hour early. He said he thought they were tired of waiting on him and decided to make him wait.

He went for radiation. Someone came and told me that he had to see the doctor today and I can go in. He was waiting in a little room for the doctor to come. She came in and talked briefly. I asked when will they do another x-ray. She said not until the radiation is over, but if we wanted one they will do it today or Monday. Otis was too weak to go for an x-ray. We left and went home.

He got in the bed as soon as we got home. He is so weak. He can't walk too far. He prefers to stay in bed.

Tricey got a call from Beverly Brown. Tricey wasn't at home. Beverly told me to tell her to get her paperwork in because the principal was very impressed with her. When Tricey came in and I told her about it. She was very excited although she didn't want to work at certain schools.

Tricey, Mae, Miss Sister and I went to Ryan's Steakhouse for dinner. Otis was resting in bed. He didn't want anything to eat. His appetite is still poor. He doesn't eat anything but a little fruit and an Ensure Plus.

When we left Ryan's, Tricey went over to my mother-in-law's. I had to go out east to check on an apartment. We had tenants that wanted to move in that night, and I had to do some last-minute work. Mazella was with me. We left the apartment and went on Merrill Road to a place called Hot and Now where Stanley Green, the tenant, worked so I could give him the keys to the apartment. When he saw me, he bagged up some French fries and hamburgers. I gave him the keys, took the bag and left.

Back home, my husband's family was there, his mama and three sisters, Mattie, Jacquelyn, and Gloria. Tricey told me that I missed it because they had been crying.

When I walked in the door, Mattie and Joshua took the bag and started eating. I was still full from Ryan's. When I got home from the east side, they said that Otis was worried about me. Mattie was upset with her husband. I tried talking to her. She wasn't listening. She is very sweet and kind, and she loves her husband.

Otis was still in the bed resting. After the family left, I went in my office (the bathroom) and read my bible and my daily bread. I prayed. Then, I went to bed.

May 8

Today, I slept in. I got up and took his (Otis') vital signs. Everything seems okay. I read the pamphlet in the Pulmocare and it stated that not eating could cause weakness from lack of oxygen and Pulmocare will help, so I started Otis off with Pulmocare. He still stays in bed from weakness. He is short of breath too. I try to get him to take deep breaths. I feel he's not breathing deep enough to exchange gases in his lungs.

I called Pop (Otis' brother). We went out east to the apartment to change the stove. We were waiting for Big Man (another brother) to come from Savannah, Georgia. The tenant called to tell me they were going to be leaving the apartment soon, so I had to go out there to get the keys. After I had been there for quite some time, Pop and Big Man came with the stove. They put the new stove in and took the old one out. We then went downstairs to clean out the bottom apartment.

I called Deborah Hankerson since it was her birthday, or so I thought. I started singing happy birthday, and she asked me, "When is my birthday?" I said, "Today, isn't it?" She said, "No. It was the sixth, but I am accepting happy birthdays for the whole month of May."

- ~ Otis' urine is dark, like deep gold. I asked him to drink more water.
- ~ He had a high temperature again, but not too high.
- ~ He went to sleep and slept all night as always.

I am hoping he will feel up to going to church Sunday since it's Mother's Day.

May 9

I woke up and started preparing for church. I woke him up, and he was still really weak. I decided not to go to Sunday school. Cyn came by and Kailyn, "Ms. Live Wire." She was dressed and looking really cute. I fixed Otis a little oatmeal and gave him a can of Pulmocare. He ate that and laid down.

I got myself ready and slipped out the door from Kailyn. I went up to the church to get DeAndrea, Trey, and Adrienna. On Mother's Day, I usually take all the grands to church with my mother-in-law.

After church, some of Otis' cousins and aunts came by to see him. He was too weak to come out of the room. They came in the room to see him. His breathing is really short. He can't stand or sit too long. All he wants he wants to do is sleep. His mother and baby brother and sisters came by too.

Later that afternoon, Tricey prepared dinner for me. She cooked a steak and baked a potato. She sautéed onion, bell pepper, and mushrooms in garlic and butter. When I looked at the sautéed vegetables, I said, "I know I'm not going to eat this."

I did not get a chance to eat until very late. Our sons and their wives came by to see us and collect their children. Tricey had been nice and fed them earlier. It was getting late and she had to get on the road to Tallahassee.

This is her last term. We are looking forward to her graduation.

For Mother's Day, Tricey bought me a beautiful dress and Otis had her to get me a beautiful watch from him. Deborah and Tony bought me a nice gown. Trey and Cyn gave me a nice card and told me I'll get a gift later.

Tina bought me a card too.

Tricey left home about 5:20 pm and called me about 8:15 pm. Mazella called a little later to see if she had called.

Gail and Judy had been over earlier and stayed until dark.

Otis is in the room quiet, watching T.V. I felt his skin. It was warm. I took his temp and it was up. I gave him Tylenol. Later in the night, I took his temp again. Before going to bed, I took it again and it was normal.

He has so many medications. I am trying to keep them together.

I gave him a bed bath. I asked him how he was doing, and he tells me he is tired. I asked him if he was just tired or if he means he's giving up. He says he's just tired.

I pray and anoint myself with oil. I need strength. I guess I'm scared, not knowing what's really going to happen and knowing that God is in control.

May 10

Kailyn is here early. I get her and lay down again knowing I need to be up getting ready for Otis to go to radiation.

I sleep a few minutes.

The phone rings. It is Frances. We talk, and she prays.

Kailyn woke up when Otis started coughing. I feed her and give her a bath and dress her. I got Otis up and washed his face. He brushed his teeth earlier.

I gave him a small portion of oatmeal. Kailyn tried to eat that. As soon as he finished eating, he wanted to lay down and I tell him we have to go. He says just five minutes. I let him have ten. Then, I helped him get dressed.

He went to the car. I got Kailyn's bag ready, put the car seat in the car. She was on the other side of the car looking for me, about to cry. I had to go get her. She got in the car and decided she wanted to sit on the other side. I had to get in the car and put her in the car seat. We are late. I have to stop for gas. I saw Willie Scott. I got the gas and kept going.

We go to Baptist Cancer Center for Otis' radiation therapy. I put him off at the door and go park the car. When I came in, he was sitting quietly, still weak and short of breath.

They take him in the back and I start looking for the slip for the x-ray he is to have today. I can't find it. I remember. I left it in my tablet. I go in the back and tell them I forgot it and they say no problem. They give us another one.

Kailyn walked over to some people in the waiting room and just stared at them. I wondered if she saw they were a little lighter complexion (white). I told her to speak and come back

Otis came out and sat in the chair. He told me they were going to bring us an x-ray order slip. When the nurse came, we asked for a wheelchair because the building was next door. The nurse was nice and pushed him over there for me while I carried Kailyn and the old x-ray films.

When they finished, I went to get the car. He got out of the wheelchair and walked to the car. We went home. Kailyn went to sleep on the way home.

I got home and called Mama Collins to see if she was home, so I could take Kailyn to her because I had to go out east again. Otis got in the house, and I got something to drink, and I left. I took Kailyn in the house at Mama Collins' and put her in her little bed.

I talked with Mama C for a little while and left and went to the store. I got home, fixed me a sandwich and sat down to look at T.V. At 1 p.m., I left home to keep my appointment with the contractors and mortgage company for inspection of the apartment on Franklin Street. We couldn't get the keys to work, so I signed the papers that everything was okay.

Earlier, when we first got home from the cancer center, Otis was coming in the door so tired and weak, but I asked him for a big hug. When he did it, I felt good just being in his arms, even though they are weak.

When I got home from the apartment, there was a message from Dr. Luke's office for Otis to call them back. I called the office. The answering service was on. Dr. Luke called me and told me that the x-rays that were taken at the diagnostic center next to the cancer center show that fluid was in the lungs. Dr. Luke wanted Otis to go to the hospital. He stated that we could wait until tomorrow or go tonight. I felt that it would be better to go tonight because he wasn't breathing well.

I cooked, fed Miss Sister and ate. Deborah and the children came by. Trey came over. Earlier, Deborah brought a wheelchair from the upper room for us to use to take Otis out in the fresh air and sunshine. As I was eating, I heard Deborah and Trey back there praying with Otis. I could feel the anointing coming from back there. Adrienna tried her best to go back there, but I wouldn't let her. DeAndrea and Adrienna were eating from my plate. De said she was hungry. Deborah told me she had already eaten.

Deborah called Tony and told him we were going to the hospital, and he should come down. He came, and as usual, he ate and fixed De a plate.

Otis blacked out earlier while coughing like he did in February when he first got sick.

We left for the hospital at about 8:45 pm. Tony followed in his car. Trey asked if I wanted him to go since Tony was going. I said no, so he went home.

Before I left home, I called Margaret, Pop's wife and told her to tell Pop we were going. I called Baby Sister. She wasn't home. Her husband James said he would tell her. She called before I left to see if I wanted her to come to the hospital with me. I told her no. Tony was going with me. I called Flammie. She started to cry and asked if I wanted her to come. I told her no and to stop crying. By that time, I was crying too. I tried to reassure her that everything was going to be all right. Then, I called Bay. I thought I had calmed down, but I started crying again and she started crying and asking me where her brother was. I had to get myself under control and tell her he was okay and that we were going to the hospital.

Earlier, when I told Otis about the call from the doctor, I told him we had to talk. He needed to tell me where everything was in case he gets too sick couldn't tell me anything. He told me I didn't need power of attorney because the law gave it to me since I am his wife. He told me that I was the beneficiary, so I won't have any problem. The only thing he had not done was turn in the papers for the 401k that will divide it among the children and me equally. I told him he didn't have worry about that. He also told me not to spend the money too fast and in six months not have anything to live on. He also told me what apartments to sell and what house to sell.

At the hospital, they took him back to the ER. while I filled out papers. When I was finished with the papers, they told me and Tony to wait out in the waiting area and they will come for us when they finished working him up.

As we sit here, I start to write in my book. Tony wanted to know what I was writing. I told him I was writing a book. He wanted to know what it was about, and I told him, it is about what is happening.

When we first got to the hospital, the security guard got a wheelchair and pushed Otis into the ER. Tony asked if I wanted him to park the car. I told him to go with his daddy.

In the waiting room, I saw Tony was getting sleepy. He told me he was going home and gave me his work phone number. I sat there writing in my book. Some scary movie was on T.V. Reggie, one of the workers at the hospital (Sister Griffin's son), came in and we started talking. I asked about his mama and daddy. He said, "Where do I know you from?" I told him Philippian.

It was getting late and they had not come out yet. Reggie went to the back to see what was going on. He came back to tell me I could go back there and the attendant at the desk told me at the same time.

Otis was sitting at the foot of the stretcher bed. Oxygen was on with a nasal cannula. He was breathing better. We had time to talk while we were waiting for his room. He told me not to worry about him. I told him, "All I want to know is that you know Jesus and that He's in your life." He said yes.

I was a bit confused about what he wanted the children to have just in case he didn't make it, so he told me again the 401k is to be divided four ways.

I told him he didn't have to worry about that.

Dr. Lesense came over and told us the room will be ready in about thirty minutes. She told us about the fluid in the lungs. Then, she called me outside and asked me if the doctors had told us just how bad it was. I told her they had told us it was cancer, but not too much more. Also, I told her there had been some change in the film and that it looked better. She told me that his cancer was in the last stage and that he may not make it home again.

When she first called me out, I looked up and said, "Lord, help me." I am so glad I did. I was able to hear what she said without falling apart.

When I went back in with Otis, he wanted to know what she said. I told him she wanted to know if the doctors had told us what was going on. I didn't tell him she said he might not make it home. It took all the strength I had not to start crying and yelling.

He and I talked some more as we waited. I told him how Verdell told Harry he had gone to glory before her. Otis smiled and said, "It be that way." I said, "Yes, one has to leave the other." I told him how Pastor Callahan said he hopes he and Sister Callahan can go together. Otis said that would be nice. Me and him together.

May 11

They finally came to carry him to his room. That was a long walk down dark corridors. Reggie had been called to help transport Otis.

On the floor, at about 12:35 am, they asked me to wait in the waiting room.

I sit here writing in my book (tablet) thinking about what the doctor had told me. I had called Otis' pastor, Rev. Joe Calhoun earlier while in the ER waiting room. His wife asked if I needed him to come to the hospital now and if someone was with me. I told her my son was with me and no he didn't need to come. She told me to call any time of day or night if I needed them.

As I sit here in the waiting room, I just thought about us, how we had misunderstood each other due to lack of communication. He felt that I was fighting against him. I thought he didn't like me and was just mean to me. So much time wasted, and unless the Lord intervenes, there's very little time left.

I had prayed earlier and told the Lord I didn't want him to suffer. I thank God that he's not in any pain, or so he says to me. He still has the faith that everything is going to be all right.

The nurse, Rush, came to the waiting room to get me. In the room, 314, Otis told me not worry about him and for me to go home. We had prayer together and I kissed him and left the hospital about 2 am. It was a funny, eerie feeling driving home that late or early in the morning with his clothes in a bag.

At home, I hung up his pants, put his money and wallet up. I called the insurance company back because they had left a message on the machine. I was told that a nurse would call me back.

I washed dishes and straightened up the kitchen. The nurse called back from the insurance company. I told her about Otis being admitted and the diagnoses. She told me everything will be all right.

I fixed me a cup of tea and went into the bathroom to read my bible. I read, and I prayed. I prayed for Otis to live, that the Lord will give us more time together to love each other and to love and praise the Lord together.

I finally went to bed at about 3:15 am.

7:30 am

Mazella called to check on me. I told her what the doctor in ER had told me. She was upset. She said she wished he had enjoyed his life more. Then, Margaret called, and I told her. She said she will come by or see me later. Deborah called to have prayer with me and to encourage me to come to noonday prayer. I was strengthened by the prayer. Baby Sister had called too. I was crying after I told Mazella everything. It just seemed that my world was crumbling down.

I know that God is in control and that all I need to do is trust in Him, but it is so hard to do when I see Otis short of breath.

8:30 am

I got up and prayed for strength and thanked God for saving Otis and healing his body. I was so sure He was going to do it.

I made me a cup of coffee and got ready to go to the hospital. I waited until about 10 am before leaving for the hospital. I called Deborah to tell her that I was not coming to prayer, but I will be at church tonight.

At the hospital, I walked in the room and he was sleep. He looked better. The oxygen was making him feel better and breathe better. I made sure it was okay for me to be in the room with him.

Then, I went to the car and got the tape player, so I could play a tape that Deborah had given us about Jairus' daughter's healing. He slept and listened. He said he didn't sleep well last night. I played the tape anyway knowing it can reach into the subconscious mind while he was sleeping.

While we were listening, Elder Jones and Elder Trice came by and had prayer. Pop came by too. Elder Jones said he was up in the prayer tower praying and calling out Otis' name when Deborah came up and told him that Pastor wanted him to go to the hospital to pray for Otis. Elder Jones says that was a not coincidence. It was God. He prayed in the room and he told us they came to heal. He started talking about Jairus' daughter that Pastor had preached, and I told him, and Otis told him too, "That's what we were listening to." When Otis said something, that let me know he had heard the tape too, even if he was sleep. I prayed it entered his spirit. Elder Jones prayed for life and healing for Otis.

It was a blessing to feel the anointing. They left, but God's presence was still in the room.

Otis talked to Pop about taking time to enjoy his self, spending some money, and going on trips. Pop said, "I thought you told me to save." He told him, "Yes, but set aside some for pleasure too." Pop soon left.

Now, it's just me, Otis and the Lord. I turned the tape on to finish listening.

The buzzer goes off. The nurse comes in to reconnect the leads. The tape is off.

Otis is asleep, so I'll watch the soap operas.

About three o'clock, Dr. Luke came in and wanted to know if the tube had to be placed in the lung. He left and talked to the nurse. The nurse came in to tell us about the procedure and place the tray in the chair. She told us that Dr. Stilt will be in, in about thirty minutes, to do the procedure.

I decided to go home to check on Miss Sister and feed her, so I can get back and spend some time with him before going to church. I stopped at Popeyes and bought some chicken and came home.

Sometimes, during the day I read a scripture concerning David's son. It reminds me of how David fasted and prayed for him until he died. Then, he strengthens himself and went about his normal routine. I said to myself I must fast and pray for Otis.

I don't want him to die.

As I was preparing to feed Miss Sister, Mae came by. She talked and ate with us. We talked about Otis and what the doctor had said. She was hurt, and tears came into her eyes. Mae went home, and I went back to the hospital.

Otis was resting quietly. The tube was draining. He told me they had gotten two bottles of fluid from the lung. When the nurse saw me, she called me outside to tell me she had given him something for pain and didn't want him to talk. She also told me about the fluid they removed, about 2,600 ccs.

I went back in the room and put the tape he wanted to listen to in the tape player. I told him not to talk, but to breathe deeply. As he listened to the tape, I set in a chair thinking about the fluid they had got out. No wonder he was short of breath. I went to sleep.

Deborah came in and sat with us. At about six, Tony and Baby Sister came in. The nurse told them not to stay long. Deborah and I went out, so they could visit since he is in Intensive Care. Flammie was in the waiting room. I told her to go on in. Deborah and I just sat and talked. Tony and the others came in the waiting room and sat down.

I told Tony that Herbert our neighbor was down the hall. Just at that time, I saw Gloria, Herbert's daughter-in-law. I asked what room he was in, and she told me. She was looking for the bathroom and walked passed it. I went to see Herbert for a few minutes. Ruth and Harry were in the room. Herbert was sitting up trying to eat.

I went back to the waiting room and Deborah told me to tell Tony what the doctor told me last night. Flammie and Baby Sister were there, and I just looked at Deborah because I didn't want to tell them anything right then. The both of them got up crying and left. I told Tony that the ER doctor told me that Otis might not make it home. Then he asked questions about the situation. I answered to the best of my ability.

It was getting late, so I went back in to talk with Otis before leaving for church. He still seemed to be in good spirits. He asked if everyone had gone. I told him Baby Sister and Flammie had gone but Tony and Deborah were still out there. I left after kissing him and telling him that I love him. I told Deborah and Tony to go back and say bye. Deborah went, but Tony said, "I've seen him already." I told him I didn't care if he had. Go back and say bye. Deborah and I left him sitting there.

I told Deborah I know he (Tony) was hurting, He didn't know how to handle this. I told her I will see her at church.

I went to my mother-in-law's house. I knew Baby Sister, Bay and Flammie were there. I told them everything the doctor had told me. They all were crying, and so was I. My mother-in-law said, "He is in God's hands."

I called Tricey and told her he seems to be doing better. She knew he was in the hospital because she had called Deborah at the prayer tower. I didn't tell her what the doctor said because I didn't want her upset while in Tallahassee in school by herself. She told me she would be home this weekend.

I left and went to church. The message was good. It was about the woman interceding for her child, and how we can pray for our loved ones. He also mentioned the scripture that had come to my mind earlier about David's son.

After the message, I went to the altar to pray. Pastor Callahan laid hands on me and the Lord blessed. I was releasing my faith to God for Otis' healing.

After church, as I was leaving, I spoke to Freda, and she told me she had been disobedient because the Lord had given her something to tell me when she called earlier, but I was in a hurry and she didn't tell me, but Pastor had talked about it in the message. I told her that he had spoken on one scripture that I had thought about today, too. I asked her to tell me what her scripture was, and she said about David fasting and praying for his son. I told her that was the one the Lord had placed on me today or rather it had come to my mind.

I decided that I am going to fast and pray for Otis like never before.

My niece Robin called a little before 12 am. She told me Tricey had called her and told her about Otis being in the hospital. She told me to tell Otis that she loves him and is praying for him. Also, she told me that she is about five weeks pregnant. I asked when will the baby be born. She said January. I told her it will be snowing, and I am not coming. She said she will have to go this one alone then.

She doesn't care if it is a boy or girl, just as long as it is normal and healthy.

She says her daddy (Nathaniel, my brother-in-law) was doing okay.

May 12

It is now about 12:35 am and I am tired and sleepy, so I am going to get a cup of tea and read before I go to bed.

I did do some reading before going bed. I read about how David fasted and wept for his child and after the death of the child, he strengthened himself and did eat. I felt I was really being led to fast and pray for my husband. Also, I have mixed emotions because of the outcome of David's son. I don't know what will happen to my husband, but I will have the satisfaction of knowing I stayed before the Lord on his behalf.

I love my husband, but I don't want him to suffer. I prayed the other night for the Lord to give us another chance to be with each other and Him (the Lord).

I was awakened this morning by a phone call from Eileen. She was calling to check on me. I thank God for Eileen. She is a blessing to us. She went to work this morning at the church, so Mama Collins can keep Kailyn. She was telling me also that Debra Brown asked about me.

I went back to sleep. I felt tired. I woke up at about 8:35 am. I got down on my knees and I prayed. I prayed for my husband, that the Lord will let him live. I also asked God to sanctify the fast.

As I was trying to get ready, Mae and Mama Collins called to see how things were going.

I left home at about 10:00 am to go to the hospital. Pop was there with Otis when I arrived. Pop said Minister Jones had already been there. He said Minister Jones told them that he and Pastor were at McDonald's and they started talking about Otis. Pastor told him to go to the hospital and pray. Also, Otis said Rev. Calhoun had been there.

Otis looked good. He was breathing better. He said he felt better.

Pop said the doctor came in and was surprised when Otis didn't want anything for pain. While I was in there, the nurse came in to see if he needed anything for pain. Bay came in and talked with him for a while. Pop left. Bay and I talked, and Otis told her to just go someplace and get a job and stop talking about doctors. I think she just said something to get him fussing. Bay stayed and talked for a while and then left.

So many things are happening that I forget them. Like this morning when Deborah called, she called to pray with me and to encourage me. It is so good and nice to know that you have people praying with and for you. I stayed at the hospital until almost 12 noon.

Otis told me to leave and go to the beauty parlor for a hairdo. Before I left, I asked him if he was going to leave me (die). He said, "Oh no. We are going to have some fun."

~ They came to do an ultrasound of his heart.

At the beauty shop, I was early. I sat down and started to write, and Ms. Smith came in. As she was doing my hair, Beulah Williams came in. I told her about Otis being in the hospital again and what the ER doctor told me. Also, I told her about Robin being pregnant.

When I finished at the shop, I came home to get Miss Sister something to eat and check on her. She gets so lonesome here by herself, but what can I do? I want to be with my husband. He needs to stay encouraged and prayed up.

After Miss Sister ate, I left again. I stopped by the bank for a computer printout. At home, there was a message on my answering machine that Annie Mae, a friend of mine, had passed. I called her son and talked briefly to him. He said he was all right. I also told him about Otis and told him to call me if he needed me to do anything.

I saw Minister Jones at the bank. He told me he ministered to Pop. Otis was encouraging Minister Jones on like he wanted him to get Pop. I know Pop seemed impressed by Minister Jones.

When I got to the hospital, they were doing something in the room, so I walked around to see Herbert. I was told by the nurse they were going to transfer him to the fourth floor. Herbert was glad because he felt he was closer to going home. When I got back to Otis' room, he was lying there resting. He looked at me and told me I looked pretty.

I ran into my friend Barbara downstairs. She told me they had just taken her aunt, Kathy, over to hospice.

As I was sitting there, Otis' dinner came. He ate pretty good. Tony and Baby Sister came. As I talked to Baby Sister, Tony talked to his daddy. I think I heard him tell Tony he had some pain or something. He had told me differently. He did tell me he needed something for pain where they left the tube in. I think he tries to keep things from me, so I won't worry. I did get the nurse to bring him a pain pill.

Ruth and Harry came in to see Otis on their way to see Herbert.

Otis was telling them that it is good to know you have people praying for you. They left wishing him well. Tony soon left also. I told him I think I will leave early too. Baby Sister and I talked some more as he watched the news. Trey came in and sat down to talk to his daddy. They really had a conversation going like he and Tony did. Baby Sister left. I told her I was coming right behind her. I stayed a little while longer, until a little past eight. I kissed him and Trey. Then, I left.

I got home just as Miss Sister was closing the drapes. I came in my room and prayed and thanked God for his blessing before getting something to eat. I decided to call Barbara to check on Kathy. She wasn't home, so I called her mother's (Sharon) house. Sharon told me they were all at her grandmother's. So, I asked Sharon how Kathy was. She told me that Kathy died at 8:00 pm tonight. I called over to her grandmother's house and talked to her (Ethel), to let them know I was sorry to hear about it. Ethel said Kathy had been really sick. I think they were relieved some because Kathy had been at home with her mama and suffering so long.

I made phone calls as I prepared my dinner. I talked to Loretta and Mae. Eileen called just as I was finishing dinner. We talked a long time about the scriptures and how the Lord was working through my husband's sickness. I washed dishes and put the trash out.

Tricey called and talked for about 15 minutes. The L.C. Callahan ministry came on. I sat down to listen and write in this tablet. The pastor was ministering that the fervent prayer of the righteous availeth much.

Now, I am going to get a cup of tea, read the bible and pray before I go to bed.

I decided to call my sister Deborah before reading. We talked for a long time. She says she is doing all right. She also told me that Otis had come before her and she prayed for him. I know the Lord did that because he is sick, and we need all the prayer we can get.

May 13

I was awakened by a phone call from Frances. I had slept all night. I didn't even wake up to go to the bathroom. Frances prayed, and the

Lord blessed. I felt lifted in the spirit. After the prayer, I got up and started trying to get ready to go out to the hospital. The phone kept ringing. I couldn't get ready. I wanted to get to the hospital in time to give Otis his bath and see the doctor. I finally got there at about 10 am.

I gave him his bath. He sat up in a chair. The chest tube is still in, pumping fluid from his lungs. The doctor came in and told us that he wouldn't take the tube out yet because it was pumping too much fluid for him to put the medicine in. He also said that Otis is doing better than he was. We can see that.

The heart doctor, Dr. Dean, came in and told us there was no fluid around the heart, but the heart is a little abnormal, but that was the least of our worries right now. Now, we are more concerned about the tumor in the lungs.

I left the hospital to go home to get some clothes to go over to Mae's house to wash them. I took Miss Sister with me. She enjoyed getting out of the house. I started the clothes, but I could not get the machine to do right.

Earlier at the hospital, I played a tape called The Invisible Instructor. Pastor Callahan was really preaching. Otis was enjoying it. He was amening along with Pastor. The anointing was very high. Then, Pastor and Keith were singing the song, "Give Thanks." The anointing and praise on the tape were electrifying. A lady on the dietary staff came in and she started moving with the music and singing. Manda and Gladean came in. Gladean prayed and we talked about the goodness of God. Otis was saying, "Let the redeemed of the Lord say so."

Mazella came home and got the washing machine going. She also went and got something to eat for us. Tricey called over to Mae's and I told her that I was going to the hospital. I dropped Miss Sister back at the house and came back to the hospital. Mazella's neighbor, Ms. Johnson was brought to the hospital this morning and she was on the same floor with Otis. We stopped by her room to see her. She was doing okay. She said she was ready to go home before she got here. We went on to Otis' room. He was back in bed. He said he feels okay.

He is still looking okay. Tricey came to see him. He told me that Jimmy and Johnson, his coworkers, had come by. Tricey got ready to go and Mazella went with her. I stayed until about eight. I got up to go and I decided to pray. As I was praying, I felt a hand on my shoulder. I wondered who it was, but I didn't stop praying. Soon, I heard a voice and realized it was Trey.

When I left, I went back to Mae's to finish washing clothes. Then, I looked at the T.V. ministry again. After the ministry was off, I went home. At home, I fixed a cup of hot tea, read my bible and went to bed. Sister Adkins called this morning early to see if she can come to the hospital to see Otis.

May 14

I was awakened again by the phone. It was Frances calling. Again, I had slept all night. Frances and I talked some and then she prayed. I got up and started getting ready to go to the hospital. I prayed also asking God to sanctify the fast. God is so good, and I am thanking Him for Otis' healing and for His mercy on us.

I got to the hospital and gave Otis his bath. He wants to stay in bed today. He looks a little weak today. He says he <u>thinks</u> he's feeling all right. The doctor had been in already. He said, "The doctor says he is going to let the tube stay in a little longer."

Pop came, and we just sat and talked. Tricey came in too. Deacon Brooks came by to see Otis and Clarence Yates came also. We all talked for a while.

Later, Pop said he was thinking about Minister Jones. Otis told him it was Friday, he is supposed to go to church tonight. Otis told me that Minister Jones and Minister Mincey had come out to pray for him this morning. I told Pop he should come to church. I asked him if he was afraid. He walked out the door. I followed him and told him it was not a coincidence that Minister Jones came on his mind today. I told him it was God. Earlier, he said we stay in church too long. I told him to sit where he can go out without disturbing anyone if he needs to leave before church is out.

Otis got something for pain at the site of the tube. He went to sleep.

I'm sitting here writing and looking at him. It is hard just looking at him. His breathing doesn't seem as easy as it was on yesterday. Earlier, Sister Adkins came by and brought a plant. She also gave us scriptures to read. She also gave me some anointed oil. She says it was fresh off the press from Pastor Callahan. She told me to anoint Otis with the oil and read Isaiah 45 to him. She also gave me a scripture, Isaiah 41:10. I anointed him and read to him. He ate lunch late because he had eaten breakfast late.

Dr. Luke came in. He looked at fluid and said he would probably take the tube out tomorrow. He said he had talked to Dr. Stilt about it.

It is 4:30 pm. Otis is sleeping, snoring even. The nurse just came in and took his vital signs. His temperature was 99.9. It had gone up. He seems to be breathing better right now.

I can't let my hopes go down. I have to keep the faith that God is going to raise Otis up. Sometimes, I get anxious or afraid that he is not going to make it. I love him, but I don't want him to suffer. I still have hopes that God is going to heal him. I thank God for that.

I looked at Otis earlier and I told him to tell me that he loved me. He looked me in the eyes and said, "I love you, baby." I told him, "Thank you." I told him that I was going to church tonight, and he said, "That's good."

I'm leaving the hospital now to take Miss Sister and Mae to dinner. I don't know if Tricey is going or not. Otis is still sleeping. I must wake him to kiss him and let him know that I am leaving.

I love him so much. I wish there was something more I could do for him.

We had dinner at Ryan's Steakhouse. The food was good, but I didn't eat much as I usually eat. Tina came by Ryan's and had dessert with us. I think I ate least because I've been on a fast. The people sang Happy Birthday to Miss Sister. Her birthday is tomorrow.

After eating, I dropped Mae off and went to church. The Lord really blessed. Pastor Callahan was preaching about the origin of the church and the obstacles we have had since conception. He prayed for people throughout the church, and he was saying, "It's going to be all right." He wasn't laying hands. He was placing his arms around them as in a hug. The anointing was so great. As he prayed for me and placed his arm around my neck, he begins to say, "It's going to be all right." I felt the power of God. I felt that everything is going to be all right with Otis.

When I think about it being all right, I have to think about it like this: there are two ways it can be all right. It can be all right in death when you die in the Lord, or it can be all right when the physical healing takes place. I know God can do both. All I can do is pray and hope that God allows the physical healing to be in His will.

I didn't get home from church until 12:30 am, BUT I felt good in the Lord. I had my tea, read my bible, prayed and went to bed.

May 15

I woke up at 7:15 am. I got up and checked on Miss Sister (Ida Mae Brown). She was almost dressed for her birthday breakfast at Shoney's. I woke Tricey up and went to get ready myself. Barbara Jean called for me to come get her for Annie Mae's funeral. We went to breakfast. They sang happy birthday to Miss Sister and give her cake and ice cream, which we all ate.

I left there, dropped Miss Sister off at home with Tricey and went to the hospital. Tricey told me before I left that Annette Bell, Otis' classmate, had called. Tricey called her back and left a message on her answering machine for me.

At the hospital, Otis was quiet. I had to do most of the talking. He was sleeping. I was wondering if they were snoring him. That's when they keep them sedated when they are in pain and about to leave here.

The doctor came in with Tricey and I there and ordered medication to put in the chest tube. He told us he was going to clamp it off and put medicine in the tube. The medicine is supposed to keep the fluid from accumulating again.

Otis asked him what could he expect to happen. "Will there be pain?" He explained that they will give him Xylocaine[9], a local painkiller. Tricey and I left so we could go to the funeral.

---

[9] A local numbing agent used to reduce pain during medical procedures

At the church, Tricey, Barbara Jean and I went to view the body. They got there first because I was speaking to everyone. At the casket, I looked at Annie Mae. She looked almost as she did when we were young, so peaceful yet it saddened my heart that she was gone, and I could feel the tears welling up in my eyes. I stood there for a long time just looking. I know God allows things to happen, but she could have taken better care of herself. Being a nurse, she knew the danger signs about her kidneys malfunctioning. I took my seat just near the casket. It was her turn to be in the front. We had worked in this church together for a long time since we were young teenagers. That is until I left.

The ceremony started. The family came in. WJ came in a wheelchair with Jamie pushing. Peanut, Joyce, Sha and the others came after. The family viewed the body as they came in. WJ was pushed to the side as everyone viewed. They finally stopped everyone and pushed him to the casket. He placed his hand on her face and just cried.

I thought about everyone expecting him to transition (pass away) first because he was so sick. He had lost his eyesight years ago. Then, he had a stroke.

Annie Mae worked hard at being successful. She worked too hard. She got sick. Her kidneys failed, and she still tried to work and take care of him. It was suggested that she put him in a nursing home. She would not think about it. When she had a stroke, she ended up in the nursing home because there wasn't anyone to take care of her. He was home, yet she ended up in the same nursing home where she was the director of nurses.

> When you are in pain and hurting for a loved one, make yourself stay connected with God.

As I sat there in the service, tears kept coming to my eyes. Cheryl sang a solo, "God Will Take Care of You." The song is so true. Sometimes, when you are in pain and hurting for a loved one, you have to make yourself really stay in touch with God.

As the different people read different church things, one sister got up and said, "As Deacon Wright said, ...". I kind of got upset before she could finish because I felt she had a thing for my husband. I didn't just start to think that way. It's been happening a long time. She immediately apologized for the mistake of calling out my husband's name and kept speaking.

After the funeral, I came home, changed clothes and was about to leave when Deacon Stephens stopped by. He talked to me about the will of God for Otis. We talked about things I have already thought about, and I do know in my heart that God's will, will be done.

I dropped Barbara Jean off at St. Stephens AME Church on the way to the hospital.

Otis was sleep when I arrived. His mouth was open. I got a funny feeling that this may be it. I touched him. He opened his eyes and said, "Hey baby." He looked at me briefly and went back to sleep. I went to the desk and asked the nurse how Otis was doing. He said, "Otis is doing fine." They had given him medication for pain after they worked on the tube. The nurse told me, "He is just sleeping."

He slept long and hard. He opened his eyes and spoke whenever someone came into the room. Tricey and Flammie came. We just sat in the room and talked. Sister Hooks came and sat with me for a long time. Tricey and Flammie left soon after she arrived. Otis opened his eyes and said, "How are you doing, Sister Hooks?" Then, he went back to sleep. She and I talked about losing loved ones and how you are never prepared. As she was leaving, he opened his eyes and told her, "Thanks for coming." I stayed in the room for a while, then told him I had to leave because DeAndrea was in a recital tonight. He said okay. I asked if there was anything I could do before I left. He said he better urinate because he had been doing a lot of that with the IV going. I gave him the urinal and he urinated quite a bit.

His vital signs looked good on the monitor. I kissed him and told him I will be back later if the program didn't last long or that I will see him in the morning. He told me thanks for all I had done. I asked him, "For what?" He said, "For all you have done from the beginning until now." I asked him if he was thinking about leaving me and he said no. I told him if he decides he wants to leave, he had better wait until I was there, and he said okay.

If it should come to that, I don't know how I am going to take it. I know God is on my side and He will make everything all right.

I kissed him again and left.

When I got home, Tricey was doing DeAndrea's hair for the recital. It looked pretty when she finished. She also put lipstick on her and did her nails after I washed her off. Deborah came and finish dressing her. I dressed and picked Mae up.

The recital was nice. DeAndrea did well. She had to model a bathing suit and came out acting shy. Tony filmed the program. He had been to see his daddy, and there were quite a few in the room. They were asked to limit the number of visitors in the room to two at a time.

Before I left the hospital, Otis and I had prayer. It seemed that he was a little low in spirit. He perked up some before I left. This morning, he asked me to pray for him as I was going on my way.

After the recital, I gave Tricey money to get pizza. Deborah, Tony, and the kids stopped by with my invitation and ate pizza too. Tony had the video going as we ate pizza and sat around. On the tape, we saw DeAndrea perform. Adrienna decided she would perform too. She walked and turned like the models did tonight. She did well for her age. Then DeAndrea started walking and twisting like the girls did in the show. I told her she could just stop now. Tricey and Tony told her she had her chance.

May 16

It is late now. I still have to read and drink my tea. It is 1:00 am on my dead brother Isaiah's birthday. He would be in his fifties if he had lived. He has been dead for ten years now. I still think about him.

I am going to read now. Maybe the Lord will speak to me in His word.

Last month, I thought I heard the Lord say he is going to heal him, but He has to work something in Otis first. At the beginning of Otis' sickness, I thought I heard him say He was working on my behalf. I know I just have to trust God, because He is God all by his self and doesn't need any help from me.

7:30 am

Again, I was awakened by the phone. Frances called to see how I was doing and to have prayer with me. The prayer was very uplifting. I got off the phone and started preparing for the hospital. I prayed too and asked God to sanctify my fast for my husband's healing in the name of Jesus.

At the hospital, Otis was sleep. He woke up and said, "Hey baby," and went back to sleep. I asked him if he wants to listen to the tape by Kenneth Hagan that Tony had left last night. He said yes. I put the tape in the recorder, and it started playing. I thought he was sleep. Later, I asked him if he heard the scriptures and what Kenneth Sharp Hagan said about healing, and he said yes.

In his room, I sat in the chair and read the newspaper. He seems more alert today. Dr. Luke came in. He said he was going to talk to the surgeon and maybe take the tube out tomorrow. It had only pumped 10 mL out in the last 12 hours and that was a good. It was cold in the room. I had to put my sweater on. We asked the nurse if he could change the temperature to make it warmer in the room. He adjusted the thermostat.

Tricey came in. I was so cold I sent her down for a cup of coffee. When she came back, I drank the coffee and was still cold. I went to get another cup.

I went up to Ms. Johnson's room and found out that she had been discharged. I then went up to Herbert's room. He said he was he was doing good. I didn't stay long because I knew the doctor was on her way in. His son Harry was in there. I talked to him briefly. He was trying to get Herbert to eat. When I came out of Herbert's room, Dr. Sharpe asked me if I had gotten him to drink something. I told her his son was trying to get him to eat.

I left and went to the cafeteria, got me another cup of coffee and went back to the room. Tricey decided to leave so she could pack up to go back to Tallahassee.

Mama and Aquarius came out to the hospital. She is concerned about her son. She kissed him and talked to him for a while. I talked to Aquarius and encouraged him to do something with his life. He said he was working with his daddy, but he wanted something more secure. While mama and Aquarius were there, Tricey came back. She and Aquarius talked, and he soon left because I told mama I would take her home.

Otis' Pastor came and pray with him. Also, our neighbor Rushon and a church member came by and had prayer with him. Tricey left for Tallahassee at about 3:45 pm. We told her to be careful after we had kissed her.

Rev. Ernest Williams came by. He is an old family friend. He had prayer with Otis also. He left because he had to go to church. I left shortly after to take Miss Sister and Mazella out to dinner. I told Otis I will be back after we eat if it wasn't too late.

We decided to have dinner at Pic and Save on Dunn Avenue. The dinner was good. I got full really fast. After dinner, I dropped Miss Sister off and went by the funeral home to see Kathy's body, but they had closed. We went on to the hospital for a few minutes.

Otis told me that Trey and Cynthia had been there. Also, Baby Sister and mama had visited too. I kissed him again and left.

As we got out at Mazella's house, a car pulled up near the house and a lady got out. Mazella was asking me who it was. I look back, and it was Earnestine Whitehurst, my God daughter's mother. I talked to her about Jesus for a while before she left.

At home, there was a card on the door and a note for me to call Leonella Black Williams of the class of '59 at Stanton High School. I had to call another classmate, Annette Bell Jackson, to get her phone number. After I talked to her, I called Lelia Mervin. She had left a note on the answering machine for me to call her. She wanted to know how Otis was doing. Her husband works with Otis at Anheuser Busch. I had called Japhetia and Karan earlier because they had left a message too. They told me to tell Otis they are thinking about him and praying for him. Trey left a message to say that Pastor Callahan said I could get some faith and healing tapes for Otis to listen to like the one called *The Word is a Medicine*.

Another classmate of Otis' called, Margaret Cumming Pipe. We talked for a long time about the goodness of the Lord and how he can strengthen you in a time of need. She knew because she had gone through something a few years back. We had never talked as we did tonight. As I was talking to her, my sister-in-law Margaret called. I told her I will call her back.

After I finished talking to Otis' classmate, the phone rang again. It was Sister Givens that used to go to Bethlehem. She called to have prayer with me. She and I talked after the prayer for quite some time about the goodness of the Lord and how he can save and heal. It was good to talk to her. She says she is going to see Otis tomorrow.

Before I left the hospital, I noticed that the fluid was coming out more than when I had left before. I forgot to that Otis sat up on the side of the bed for a long time while mama and I was there earlier. After I finished talking on the phone, I got mad, so I went to go read.

Deborah called to see how I was doing. I learned that they were not going to open the casket at Kathy's funeral.

May 17

I finished reading and looked at, or listened to, Rodney Washington on TV and wrote in my tablet before going to bed. When I woke up, I realize I had slept longer than I wanted. I had to hurry so I could get to see Otis, have the car washed, get gas in the car, and get to the funeral.

At the hospital, I ran into someone that worked in the hospital who knew Kathy's condition. We talked briefly, and she spoke to Otis before she had to leave.

When I first got to the hospital, he told me I look pretty. I had to bait him into telling me. I was saying, "You look handsome." Then, he was saying, "You look pretty." I stayed with him a little while before going to the funeral.

Elder Virgil Jones spoke at the funeral. The anointing was there. The Scripture and prayer were done by Elder Robert Trice and Elder Anthony Mincey. After the eulogy, Mother Mitchell was praising the Lord even though she had just finished having the funeral of one of her children.

At the cemetery, some of the staff from our church were there waiting. We exchanged hellos before the family arrived. I left the cemetery and went to Krystal's to get Miss Sister some burgers, and I came home. She sat down and ate.

I left and went back to the hospital. I brought a tape with me that one his coworkers had left for Otis. I asked him if he wanted to hear it. He said yes. As the pastor of the church was preaching, some of the things he said scared me. For him, it seemed the pastor was mocking the Holy Spirit and blaspheming. I don't think he realized what he was doing. You just don't mock or speak ill of God's anointed.

He talked about speaking in tongues and said that everyone wasn't supposed to get up speaking at one time because you need an interpreter. The nurse heard and said it was amazing because she had never heard a preacher say anything like that. I told her, when people are praising God and speaking in tongues, everyone is speaking to God for himself and it is fine then, and God could give someone his own interpretation. She said okay and left the room.

I read the newspaper and watched TV. Otis and I talked too. I told him I think about wasted time, and he said he thinks about it too and we may not have any more time left. I told him we are going to have some time left because he promised me we were going to have some fun.

He had not had a bath all day, and it was time for a shift to change. The new nurse came into the room introduced herself. She told us that Deborah had told her Otis didn't have a bath. I wanted to know if the nurse wanted me to give Otis a bath. I told her it was his decision. I ended up giving him his bath. I had to cut it short because one of his classmate Margaret was out there waiting to see him.

Margaret came in the room and talked with Otis. Later, Leo, Nella, and Benny came to see him. As we sit there talking, I was thinking this is the intensive care unit and only two people should be in the room. Just as I was thinking about that, our son Tony came in and the nurse came and said, "I'm leaving." She said, "As long as it was four, I wasn't going to say anything, but not five." I left the room and let his classmate David go in. I sat in the waiting room with Tony.

They finally came out and told Tony he can go visit with his dad. He went and stayed for a while. I stayed in the waiting room talking to the classmates. When Tony came out, two of them went in to say bye to Otis. Margaret and I went in when they came out. Margaret soon left. I noticed he was tired and going to sleep, and I was about to leave when Trey came in. He prayed with his daddy, and we both left together.

As we were leaving, we ran into Fred Hankerson going to see Otis.

I told him that he was resting but to go on in. Later, Fred called to tell me that he didn't wake him up. He just stood at the bed and prayed and went to the waiting room and read the Scripture and prayed some more. Fred said as he was leaving, he saw Michael Lang, the youth minister at Bethlehem going to see Otis. Also, earlier today Rev. Griffin from Bethlehem came and stood by the bed and prayed. He held Otis' hand and prayed silently. I saw tears rolling down his face.

I got home and got ready for bed. I prayed, read my Bible, and drank my hot tea.
I am still fasting and praying for husband's healing.
I pray that I am doing that right.

May 18

I woke up late again. I didn't realize how tired my body was. Again, I rushed to get ready for the hospital. I called the room where they were supposed to take Otis. A lady answered and told me she was admitted in the room the night before. I was concerned about Otis, so I called the hospital and they told me he was still in room 314 intensive care unit and in fair condition. I had been telling people he was fair, but when the hospital said it back to me, it was hard to take. I guess I wanted them to say he was fine.
The chest tubes were supposed to come out last night.

When I got to the hospital, Otis was sitting up in a chair and he had already his bath. He looked good. He didn't have oxygen on, and there were no IVs going. He told me he had a bowel movement, a small one. It had been over a week. I think he held it because he didn't want to use the bedpan.
Later, as we were trying to get a urine specimen for culture, he had to have a bowel movement again. He pulled some of the monitors apart trying to get to the commode. He had a very good bowel movement that time and again. Later, he told me his butt was hurting. I think it was because he held on to the stool so long.
When I got to the hospital earlier, they had him all packed up and ready to go to the fourth floor. He said they had him down the hall already when they found out the room had been given to someone

else.

The nurse told me that he had been nauseated earlier. His temperature also had gone up. Later, he started to cough and throw up. The nurse came in and brought towels. I could tell he wasn't feeling well. The nurse put in a call to the doctor. She later came back and gave him a Compazine IV[10] for the nausea.

He looked at me and said, "Just as you think you're getting better, this happens." I told him, "It is going to be all right. This is only a test." He said okay. I told him about a tape Minister Jones preached a long time ago. The title was, "It's only a test." I promised that I will bring that tape when I come tomorrow.

Ernestine and Patricia came by while I was downstairs getting coffee. They stayed until it was time for Ernestine to go back to work. I walked down with them to see her new car. It was pretty, a red cougar with black interior. Tina came as soon as I got back upstairs. She stayed and talked for quite some time. When she was leaving, I left too.

Otis had been trying to get me to leave before Tina came, telling me he was sorry if he had not been thinking of me but of himself. I told him it was okay because he was the star. I could not let him know how I was hurting inside thinking I might lose him.

I got home with the intention of going to church. I went and got something to eat from Popeyes and came back home. The phone started ringing and ringing. I talked from one person to the other calling to see how Otis was doing. I ended up staying home. I still didn't get into bed until late. I watched *Bread from Heaven* on TV. The anointing was high. He called people out to pray for them. I could feel the anointing. I prayed and read my Bible. I am still asking God to heal my husband.

I am going to continue to fast.

May 19

When I woke up, I called Otis. He called and told me what room he was in last night. He said he was doing okay. I got up prayed and start getting ready to go to the hospital. When I got to the hospital I

---

[10] A medicine given through a tube to treat nausea and vomiting

found out that he had been nauseated and had to have medication.

Can you imagine how I felt when he told me he had to clean himself up because he had started to vomit, and his bowels started to move too? I know this is humiliating for him. I pray that he soon stops being nauseated.

The hospital staff was nice. They brought in his lunch and asked if I wanted a tray. I thought by them asking that it was a new thing where they offer the visitor food in the room with the patient. Since I was on the fast and going to take Miss Sister to IHOP, I said no. I told Otis that I would eat with him tomorrow. He only ate a small portion of his food.

Bob Bailey came to see Otis on his lunch break. Also, sister Henry from Bethlehem Baptist Church came. Bob had prayer with us before he left. I had taken some tapes to the hospital, but we didn't get to listen to them.

Later, he got nauseated again.

- ~ His temperature is alright.
- ~ They are giving him antibiotics through IV.

He is resting quietly, watching TV.

I left to take Miss Sister to IHOP. The food was okay. We ate and left. I dropped her off home and went back to the hospital.

I forgot to mention that when I first got to the hospital this morning, I went to see Herbert and discovered that Ruth, his wife, was a few doors down from Herbert. Harry, their son, was in Herbert's room and told me he had brought his mother out there the day before. They are our next-door neighbors.

Later, when I got back to the hospital the second time, Otis was still in bed. A student studying to be a respiratory therapist came in to do his breathing treatment. Our son, Tony was in the room with us. She wanted to know who took his oxygen off, and I told her it had been off since yesterday. She got the tubing and hooked him up again. She said she did not see or know why it had been discontinued. As she listened to his lung, she said you can hear the fluid in his lungs. I didn't say anything, but she should not have told me that. She didn't know how we might take news like that when we thought it had cleared up. She asked Tony if he wanted to listen, and he said no. Tony called Deborah and soon left. I stayed to help Otis to the bathroom and back.

As the two of us were having prayer, Harry, Gloria, and Eddie came by to see Otis. We were talking about this being a neighborhood affair since Herbert, Ruth, and Otis were on the same floor. They left, and I stayed a while longer before leaving.

He seems to be okay. I am praying. I told him, this time when he comes home, it is going to be different. I can feel it all over me that he will be home and well.

At home, I talked on the phone. Calling people that left messages on the machine. It was Margaret and Alvin Hall. I didn't call Kevin and Barbara because they had called the hospital.

I stayed up to see the L.C. Callahan ministry on TV. It was really good. The title was *The Fervent Prayer of the Righteous Availeth Much*. I prayed asking God to sanctify my fast. Last night, when I prayed asking for more time with Otis, I believe I heard the Lord say 20 more years. I pray I heard that right.

We will have time to praise and serve the Lord together. Remembering what the Lord says, now I know why I feel so good and positive about him coming home well and strong.

May 20

I woke up and called Otis. He said he's okay. However, he needed underwear and pajamas. He had an accident during the night.

At the hospital, the door was closed. I heard prayer going on. Before I left home, I called the prayer towel and Deborah told me the elders had gone to the hospital. Also, I told Deborah that I wanted to sow a seed of $100 for his healing. I walked quietly into the room. Before I got in there, I had envisioned Philippian's ministers. Them and also our pastor.

Inside the room, Elder Anthony Mincey was praying. Elder Robert Trice was with him praying too. Also, there was Reverend Calhoun, Otis' pastor. They finished praying and left. I thank God for our ministers coming to see about my husband.

The hospital staff came to get Otis to go for an x-ray.

Earlier, Baby Sister came in the room and she didn't see Otis. She wanted to know where he was. I looked at her crazy, and she was scared. I told her he was in the bathroom. I also asked her if she thought I could be standing there that calm if anything had happened to him.

Pop came in to see Otis. He was happy that he looked better. While Pop and Baby Sister were there, Otis was looking in the paper and saw carpet for sale. He told them that he was going to buy some carpet. I didn't really understand what he had said, so I asked, "Who is going to get carpet?" I couldn't believe he was talking about us because I have had worn out carpet for a long time. I was ready to hop on it, but he told me to wait until we see Sunday's paper.

I have put the tape on entitled, *The Word is a Medicine,* but they were talking and did not hear it. Pop and Baby Sister left. Otis and I just sat looking at TV.

I had gone to see Herbert and Ruth when I first got to the hospital. Herbert wasn't doing too good. Ruth was sitting in a chair. They brought the lunch tray for Otis and I told the girl at the desk they could bring me a tray today. She said they just had extra trays yesterday. I was disappointed because I was looking forward to eating with him. He didn't want all his food anyway, so I helped by eating the cheese soup and bread.

We didn't do much talking today. We just looked at TV. Tricey called us from Tallahassee to see how her daddy was doing. She asked me to call Beverly Brown and ask her to tell the principal of the school that her papers should be in by Monday.

Tina came to the hospital. She didn't want to stay in the room because she had a cold and was afraid she might give her god daddy something.

Flammie came to see Otis. She sat for a while talking and looking at TV. While she was there, Alexander Jordan, one of the deacons from Bethlehem came by. When they left, I helped Otis to the bathroom before I left. He had his thermometer[11] on. His temperature was still up. They had to call Dr. Kawaaf, the infection specialist, back on the case.

Before I left, I told him we would have to listen to the tape tomorrow because we didn't hear it this morning, and he said okay. He also told me to get his tithes ready. Bring the books and a bank computer printout so he can check things over. Also, he told me he wanted to give a donation to Philippian TV ministry. I ask how much he wanted to give and he said $100. I told him I had told Deborah I wanted to give $100 this morning and I knew God was doing that because we both came up with the same thing.

I left the hospital, came home got Miss Sister, and I got clothes to go to Mae's house to wash. I got a load going and went in the kitchen and ate. Mae had cooked chicken and butter peas and white acre peas. It was so good. Miss Sister said she was not hungry, but she soon ate.

I called Otis to check on him. He told me Trey was there with him. I had dialed the number and didn't get an answer. I got a little alarmed. I hung up and dialed back. When I asked him about it, he said the phone didn't ring. I must have dialed the wrong number. He said he was okay.

I finish washing, came home and put away the clothes. Then I went in the bathroom, read my Bible and wrote in this tablet.

May 21

(entry added 6/6)

As you can see, it has been a long time since I wrote in this tablet. I'm going to try to remember what I can starting with Friday, May 21.

I got to the hospital and parked in the parking lot. I saw Earnestine and Sister Mobley Bay were leaving. I talked to them briefly before going up to see Otis. He was resting quietly. We talked and watched TV together. I told him that I was planning to give tithes to my church from the money I had gotten from the last rental property. He wanted to know how much it was. I told him it was only about $60. The week before I had taken almost $600 to his church. He looked at me and

---

[11] A device that measures a patient's temperature

said, "If that's what you want to do." We talked some more, and I left so I could take Miss Sister out to dinner.

Mazella, Miss Sister and I went to Ryan's Family Steakhouse. We ate the same as usual. I dropped Mae off and came home with Miss Sister. I don't remember what else I did that night, but I do know I prayed and read my Bible.

More From...

May 22

I remember I went to the hospital. Otis did not seem as strong. I could not put my finger on it, but I felt something was wrong. I think I stayed out there all day before coming to check on Miss Sister. I don't remember what visitors came that day.

At home, I read and prayed and went to bed.

May 23

I did not go to church. I decided to go to the hospital and be with Otis because I didn't like the way he acted the day before. As I thought about it, I remember he started acting different when I told him I plan to give tithes from the business to my church. I guess he felt that we had given a hundred dollars to my church already and didn't need to give to my church anymore. I felt we should split the tithes from our business. Anyway, I didn't give my $60 to my church.

When I got to the hospital, I told him that I didn't give the money because I felt didn't want me to. He did not say it was okay, so I knew he didn't want me to. I thought about how the Lord allowed me to know what the problem was with him (Otis). Then to let me know that God doesn't want us to give Him anything against our own will. He wants us to give willingly.

I left and came to check on Miss Sister and to feed her.

I got back to the hospital, and I saw Sister Hooks and Sister Tolbert going in the hospital. I slowed down because I wanted them to get to the room first or all of us would be going in at the same time. I parked the car and sat there for a few minutes. When I walked in the hospital door, Sister Hooks and Sister Tolbert were still standing at the check-in getting a pass to go to the room. We got on the elevator together and went up to the fourth floor. I told them how to get to the room, and I went to see Ruth and Herbert.

I sat and talked to Ruth Boyd while before going in to see Otis. When I got to the room, Sister Hooks started to pray. As she was praying, Trey came in. When she finished, I felt like just praising, and as I praised and thank God, Trey started to pray again. The Lord really blessed.

Just as we finished praying, Dr. Stephen, Otis' classmate starts in the room and backed out, and I told him to come on in. He said, "I don't want to interrupt your praying." I told him to come on in because we had finished praying. He came in and spoke with Otis Then, he said he will be back another time.

I sat with Otis after everyone had gone.

I don't remember what else happened at the hospital. I know at home I read my Bible and prayed after talking on the phone. Whenever I get home, I check the answering machine and call everyone back.

May 24

I know I called Otis as soon as I woke up. This is what I have been doing since he moved into a room with a phone. After talking to him, I prayed. I am still fasting and praying for his healing.

Ruth went home from the hospital today. Herbert was still there. It seemed that every time I go to see him, he was on the bedside commode. Whenever I saw that, I would leave the room because I didn't want him to be embarrassed. He still has oxygen on and his breathing is not good. He is short of breath.

Otis was sitting up when I went in. We looked at TV and talked. He is not eating well yet. He said he is eating what he can. He sometimes gets nauseated.

One night in the hospital, a young lady named Eva came looking for Trey. She was a respiratory therapy student. She came in the room and didn't see Otis because I was sitting on the bed in front of him. She asked if this was Mr. Wright's room. I told her yes. Then Otis told me she was the one that got saved the other night. She came back looking for Trey because he promised her a Bible. I told her she would get it.

As Trey and I were leaving the hospital later that night, we saw her. When she saw Trey, she came back and hugged him. She is from the Philippines and she is very short, shorter than me.

At home, I did my usual phone calls, read my Bible and prayed. I thanked God for how far He had brought Otis and how Otis had been given another chance.

May 25

The next morning, Otis called to tell me he had been discharged. I prayed and fasted as usual. I am praying for a total healing.

At the hospital, Otis was waiting for his clothes. He was all packed and ready to go. They brought a wheelchair to push him out with. I carried a plant that Betty Love and District 11 had bought him. He carried some of the other packages on his lap.

On the way home, we stopped by his mother's house, so she could see him. She was so happy. There were tears in her eyes. When we got home, he went straight to the bedroom and the bed saying, "It is nothing like having or being in your own bed."

Before we left the hospital, they brought his lunch in. He refused to eat saying, "I want to go home."

We had visitors that evening, and he got very tired.

My car was sounding funny. Otis had Big Money to check the oil in my car. We discovered there wasn't any oil in the car. I remembered a dream I had a few days before. In the dream, the lights on the dashboard were lit up, indicating there was something wrong. In the dream, I remember saying, "Oh Lord, not now." It seemed the car was gone, and I knew we couldn't get another one right now. I know now that it was the Lord warning me that something was wrong although the car wasn't giving me the warning as it should have.

May 30

Tricey carried Miss Sister to church. I had told her to tell Cyn to announce that Miss Sister had celebrated her 90th birthday on the 15th of May. Pastor Callahan called Miss Sister up to the pulpit and asked her to say something. Tricey said Miss Sister just said, "Halleluiah," and the whole church went up in praise. I know that made her day. They went on to just have a praise day. I was told that a lot of young people (little ones) went up for prayer in service and they were crying.

After church, Deborah came over with the girls, DeAndrea and Adrienna. De had a handkerchief in her hand that Pastor had told her to give to her granddaddy and she went straight to the room and gave it to him. De also told me that Pastor had prayed for her for real. Adrienna went to the bed to pray for granddaddy. She got up on the bed and laid hands on his forehead. Then, she got down.

The day before, on Saturday, Tricey and I went looking for furniture. We found some at Rhodes that we liked, but we had to come home and talk it over with Otis.

Today, Memorial Day is being celebrated. I seasoned the meat last night. Tony came down to cook it on the grill. All the children came over. Otis got up and went outside to sit on the porch and watch the kids play in their little pool. Kailyn loved it. She didn't want to get out. Whenever Trey tried to get her out, she would move to the other side. Once she got in the middle of the pool and just played by herself. All the other kids had gotten out. At one point, she was saying, "Bug." There was a bug in the pool, and she got it in her mouth. Trey had to get it out of her mouth.

Deborah made potato salad, and I made baked beans. Mazella came over. The dinner was good. Tricey left for Tallahassee around 5 pm. Everyone went home. I cleaned the kitchen, read my bible and prayed. Then, I went to bed.

As the days have passed, I have watched the Lord work on my husband. He is indeed a miracle. The day we got home from the hospital, I told him that we can really praise God because they had told me in the emergency room that he might not make it home. He looked at me with wide eyes and said, "I didn't know I was that sick."

June 1993

June 1

We had an appointment with Dr. Luke. Sometimes, I think they don't know what they are doing or what to do. I asked Dr. Luke if we needed to see Dr. Sharpe again. He was indecisive about it. He finally told me to take Otis back again to see if she wanted him to stay on the Proventil. After that, we were to come back to his office in a week to have chest x-rays done before our next appointment with him.

As the time progressed, Otis wasn't drinking or eating as he should. There were calls and visits from different ones. Margaret C. came by and sat with Otis and me for a long time. After Margaret left, Otis went back to our bedroom and got into bed. I could tell he was weak. He watched TV. I washed dishes, and prayed and read my Bible. I thanked God for saving Otis and for healing him.

June 2

I am still fasting and praying for Otis' healing.

Pastor Calhoun came by. He brought a watermelon. Each time he has prayed with him, Otis is not eating well. When I question him about drinking, he tells me he has drunk enough, but I can always tell he hasn't by what's left in the pitcher.

One day, early in the morning, I took Otis' vital signs, and his blood pressure was low. I called Dr. Luke's office because I was not going to give him his blood pressure medicine with a low reading. The office nurse told me to decrease the pill. I did that, but the reading was still low, so I stopped giving it to him.

He seems to rest good at night. So do I. Sometimes, I hear him when he gets up and sometimes I don't. While we were at the doctor's office on June 1, I told the doctor about the pain Otis sometimes has in his lower back. The doctor quickly got pain pills to give Otis. I took them and put them in my purse. Otis says that Tylenol eases that discomfort, so he hasn't taken any pain medication.

The doctors are confounded because he is not in severe pain and the cancer they say he has is supposed to be in the last stage. I know that it is only God that's keeping him free of pain.

Flammie and Boo came by Thursday.

June 4

I carried Miss Sister and Mazella to Ryan's Family Steakhouse.

Flammie told me when she stopped by that Boo had caught some fish, and baby sister was going to cook some and bring it to Otis on Friday. I tried to call Flammie before I left for Ryan's, so I'll know what to do. She wasn't home or at mama's. We had our dinner and came home.

When I got in the house, I found that they had not stopped by and that Flammie forgot to take the fish out of the freezer. When they did come, they had to go by Nesbit's to get Otis a fish sandwich. They stayed and talked for a good while.

Mama sat on the sofa with Otis and talked to him as he wrote her notes. When they left, I got my hot tea, went in the bathroom where my Bible was. I read, and I prayed. I am still thanking God for saving my husband and healing him.

June 5

I got up, prayed, washed up and got Otis' vital signs. Then, I fixed breakfast. He seems to be doing a little better.

It was time to collect rent, so I left him home and went to try to collect.

I received rent from one tenant. One tenant told me she had got saved at a center across from the apartment. She gave a detailed description of what happened to her. She says she could not really understand what happened, she could not express it. She seemed happy and I was happy for her.

I left there and went to Rhodes Furniture Warehouse on our side of town. I had been to the other store and was sold furniture, but I had not picked it up. I wasn't sure about it anyway. I didn't like the treatment I received over there, so I left and went by Eartha White Nursing Home to see another tenant that works there. While there, I got to see and talk to Ms. Carter. She told me if I need her to call, and she would come and sit with Otis.

I got home, and I was trying to get Otis to take his pills. This one was to be taken with food and plenty of water. He told me to put it up there and he will take it later. I told him he has to take it down while the food was still on his stomach. He got kind of ugly with me, stating he will take it after a while. I told him to take it, and I walked out of the room angry.

I was trying to do what was right for him. I know he is tired too, but I am concerned and want to do what's right for him.

As I was watering the plants in the yard, he came out and said, "I'm sorry." I looked at him, smiled and said, "Me too." He smiled. Then we start talking about the yard. I ended up raking and pulling up weeds. By the time I finished, I was tired and sweaty. I got on the treadmill to try to burn a few more calories before taking my bath. As usual, I read my bible and prayed, and talked to Otis.

Tony and the girls came by earlier.

June 6

Today is Sunday. I got up and as usual. I prayed and asked the Lord to bless my fast as I fast for Otis' healing and a closer walk with God.

I took Otis' vital signs and got his breakfast. He seems a little weak. Miss Sister had asked Trey and Cyn to pick her up for church, so she was ready at 6:30 AM and had to wait for them. After they left, I took a shower and was dressing when the idea came to me to put anointed oil on Otis from the crown of his head to the soles of his feet. As I rubbed him, I was praying for his healing, and I believed that God is doing it. We spent time just talking. He seemed to be more alive. He smiled and relaxed more.

I got dinner on before his church members started coming in. From his district, Sister Callie Wilson, and her daughters Bettye and Dorothy came with her three grandsons. Reverend Calhoun, Deacon Thompson, Sister Jenkins and Sister Brown came to commune him. We both received communion. Reverend Calhoun prayed for Otis and laid hands on him. Last Sunday, members of the male chorus came by.
After everyone was gone, Trey and Cyn stopped by to bring Miss Sister. Trey visited with his dad for a while. After they were gone, Otis rested a while before eating dinner. This morning, as I was getting dressed, it seemed the Lord was telling me to get this book up today because He is getting ready to move. I told Trey and Cyn about it.

June 7

We had an appointment with Dr. Sharpe. She looked at Otis and touched his skin and told him he was dry meaning he didn't have enough fluid in him. She immediately gave him a cup of Gatorade. She talked about being informed about him being in the hospital and told me to give Dr. Luke a note requesting a summary of the hospital discharge. I told her about a breathing inhaler that Dr. Luke wanted for Otis. She said they should leave that up to her and Dr. Luke shouldn't take him off what she had him on. She didn't remember putting Otis on one of the inhalers. It seemed she was really confused. She did tell us to go and apply for disability. She also told us to go and apply for a handicap sticker. We left there saying we don't know what to do.
We are scared. So much has happened. We decided to go to 48th and Main to get the handicapped sticker.
Back home, Otis ate pretty good.

June 8

I am still fasting and praying for a healing for Otis. On Sunday, June 6th while I was dressing, a song came to me saying, "Healing, Healing, Healing." Each time I would say the words, I could feel the

Holy Spirit. I forgot too that Sister Givens and Sister Peterson came by and had prayer with Otis and me. The Lord's presence was here.

As we got up and dressed, I took his vital signs and decided not to give him any medication. All his vital signs were good. We had a 10:30 am appointment with Dr. Luke.

We got to the building a little after 10:00 am. We had to have a chest x-ray done and bring the films with us. Needless to say, it took forever to get a chest x-ray. We sat and sat and sat. I called the doctor's office to let them know what was going on. We were finally called to the x-ray floor at about 11:30 am and were told we had about another 45 minutes to wait. As we waited, we got into a conversation with a man whose wife I knew. We talked about the goodness of the Lord, and how far He has brought Otis. The man told us how far God had brought him and his wife, Geraldine. We finally left the x-ray department at about 12:15 pm.

While we were at Dr. Luke's office, I gave the office nurse or clerk the note from Dr. Sharpe and some insurance papers. Dr. Luke came in the room. He asked Otis how he was doing. Again, we told him about the nagging ache in the lower back. He said, "Didn't I give you pain pills?" Otis told him he takes Tylenol for that. We are trying to find out what's causing the pain. Also, Otis has a rash on his face. We asked the doctor about it, and he said he didn't know. He also said Dr. Schoopel, the radiation doctor, did not want to treat Otis anymore because it was too close to the heart. He said he didn't know what to do, whether to go back to chemotherapy or what. He said they are not sure if the chemo had helped or not.

He said we have three choices. One, Otis can stop the chemo and they can treat the symptoms as they occur. Two, he can take chemotherapy via IV or three, take a chemo pill. He said he doesn't like the pill. The pill doesn't have nausea and vomiting side effects. Whatever the decision, it has to be made by Otis.

I thought about how confused they seem to be and wondered if God was working as he said and getting ready to move.

As I look back, I think about them being confused.
It was because they didn't want to tell us they had done all they could for him.

If it was today, they would put him in hospice.

We got home in time for the people to come and measure for carpet. I can't believe after twenty-one years, I am getting new carpet. The men came and measured and gave us a price and Otis told them to let him sleep on it. I heard one of them say, "After all that work." I believe they were trying to make a sale that should have been going to someone else. He gave us a card and left.

My toe is still hurting. I was going to the door to let carpet the men in and stumped my right little toe on Pop's sneakers. He was sitting in a chair by the door with his legs stretched out, and as I was trying to pass he moved them. I thought it might be broke. It was hard to move it. It hurt so bad.

I called another carpet company. They sent someone out. He measured and gave us a price. Otis liked him. We told him we would let him know. We also picked out the carpet we wanted. After he left, I ate my dinner, Popeyes Fried Chicken. That's what Otis had a taste for.

I got the kitchen cleaned, got my tea and went into my office (bathroom) to read my bible and pray. Trey called his daddy and had prayer over the phone with him.

June 9

I woke up and prayed. I'm still fasting for Otis' healing and a closer walk with the Lord.

I asked Otis how was he feeling. He says he is doing fine. I took his vital signs and gave him the heart pill. We decided to hold off on the others. Sometimes, when I see his hands shaking I give him Xanax, a nerve pill.

He ate his cereal. He put on some clothes and sat around in the living room. Mother Bright called to say she was on the way. He sat on the sofa in the living room reading the newspaper until she came. She came in praising the Lord. Otis got up to hug her. We sat down, and she talked for a while about the goodness of Jesus. Then she prayed and talked some more before leaving. Otis looked as if he really enjoyed her visit.

I looked out the window and saw another car. It was a red or maroon. I told Otis I didn't know who that was, and just as I was speaking, Josephine Reese got out of the car. She came in and sat down.

Kailyn came today. She was really busy looking at Josephine. I had fed her early, so she was ready to eat again. I fed her lunch as Otis talked to Josephine. Reverend Calhoun came by and sat for a little while too. He prayed with us. Kailyn wanted to be busy then. He left after he prayed. When Kailyn finished eating, she got in Josephine's lap and went to sleep.

I had wieners cooking for our lunch. Josephine didn't want anything. I took Kailyn and laid her down on the sofa. I fixed the hot dogs and went in the den to look at the soap operas. Otis and Miss Sister ate too. Josephine said that Trina told her to make sure she came by here to see Otis before she comes down there for the cruise.

The carpet man called for us to come in and look at something that he had in stock. We told him we would be there later in the day. Shirley, one of our tenants called about her fridge. She was upset and wanted to break her lease. I told her it would be okay. Then, she called back and said the refrigerator was working.

I went looking for Kailyn. I found her in the kitchen with a box cereal, trying to open it. I guess she was hungry. I gave her a snack. She ate it fast. She kept eating until she only had one left.

Cyn came and she had Gab, Mear, and Trey with her. Mear and Gab have grown a lot. Mear is taller than I am, and Gab is about to catch me. Trey was excited because they were going home with him.

Daddy Collins went to the urologist today for a look into his bladder. We are praying that everything will be all right.

When Cyn and the children left, Otis and I went to check on the carpet. We decided on another piece since the one we chose last night was not in stock. We ended up paying more money, but Otis was tried.

When we left there, we went to check on our tenant Shirley. She changed her mind and wanted to stay. She then asked us to help her pay her gas bill. Otis agreed to do so, but just this one time. Then she asked for new carpet. Otis said no.

We came home, and Otis decided he wanted stew beef from Mom's Kitchen. I went back to get it and go to Pic and Save for Miss Sister. When we got home, Miss Sister gave Otis a note from one of his church members, which means she had opened the door. I keep telling her don't open the door. "Do not go near the door nor the window if we aren't home," I say, but she'll do it anyway. I can't take her with me all the time. Her excuse was that she was sitting right by the door. I got the food and we ate. I put what was left in the refrigerator. The stew and vegetables, greens and lima beans, were good.

Otis and I were on US-1 earlier and saw the aftermath of a bad accident. A big semi-truck had hit a car. The car was bent from one side to the other. I prayed for the people involved. I later found out that the man and woman in the car died and the truck driver was in the hospital.

Trey came by the house on his way to the prayer tower and had prayer with his daddy. He talked to him and then left to go get on the phone for the television broadcast. As I was washing dishes, an old song came to my mind, "Don't Give Up on the Brink of a Miracle." I finished up, and it was impressed upon me to tell it to Otis. I came into the room and told him, "Don't give up on the break of a miracle." He looked at me and smiled. *Those smiles I cherished.*

I got my tea and went in the bathroom for my reading and praying. The Lord is blessing us so much. He often gives me encouragement.

I got ready for bed. Tricey called to see how everything was going.

June 10

I woke up to a phone call from Frances. We talked about Ulysses' birthday dinner plans. I went back to sleep. Mazella called to tell me she was free because the dentist canceled her appointment.

I got up and prayed. I am still fasting for my husband's healing, and our closer walk with the Lord. Frances also prayed this morning when she called.

I took Otis' vital signs. He said he felt okay. I prepared his breakfast. I got fresh water for his pitcher. He ate breakfast. He came to the front and start reading the paper.

I left, picked Mae up and went to Rhodes to look at furniture. Mae fell in love with the same set that Tricey liked.

We left there and went to People's Gas to pay a tenant's gas bill.

We had enough time to go by the other Rhodes close to the house. They had the same thing. I decided to let Tricey make the selection when she comes home. I dropped Mae off and came home. We warmed up our leftovers and ate.

By that time, it was time to go to the heart doctor. We arrived on time and waited in the office. I saw a lady come in that lived in the back-rental unit on Ardesia. I couldn't remember her name, but I heard the receptionist say, "Irene." She sat next to me, but I don't think she remembered me. I just started talking and she asked about everyone in the neighborhood.

The nurse called us in and took Otis' vital signs. The doctor came in and asked Otis how was he doing. Otis said, "I don't know. You tell me." Dr. Dean said, "It doesn't work like that. You have to tell me something."

Dr. Dean inquired about the medication Otis was on. I showed him the list that we had from his discharge papers. I told him Dr. Luke told us to cut and stop Vasotec[12] because Otis' blood pressure got low. Dr. Dean said he wanted it low, and he wasn't giving that medicine to Otis for his pressure. I started to ask the doctor if he wanted me to start giving it to Otis if his blood pressure goes up, but I didn't. He asked Otis how he had been since he wasn't taking the medicine. Otis told him he felt fine. Dr. Dean said, "If you feel okay without it, don't take it." He asked if Otis had shortness of the breath when he lies down. Otis told him no. Dr. Dean looked at the papers he had and realized he had old hospital papers and not the recent discharge summary.

He talked around everything just like the other doctors. He said he didn't know what was causing Otis' heart to beat so fast, yet he said that was not the problem right now. The biggest is the other problem (cancer). He didn't use those words, but that's what he was talking

---

[12] A medication that treats high blood pressure

about. He also wanted to know how Dr. Luke planned to treat Otis now. We told him about our choices. We told him, option one was no chemotherapy. Option two was just to treat the symptoms as they come. Option three was to have the chemo in the office or take the pill for twelve days per month.

Dr. Dean told us he will see us in six weeks. We stopped at the desk and made the appointment and left. Out in the hall, Otis threw up his hands and said, "Thank you, Lord." I told him that God had us in a position where we had to trust him. The doctors seemed confused. *I know now that they did not want to tell us it was over.*

We stopped, got some Gatorade and peanuts, and we went to the social security office to get a slip to apply for social security disability. Then, we went out to the eastside to Shirley (our tenant) to let her know the gas would be cut on tomorrow and someone had to be home. She said she would be there.

Back home, Otis was talking about tomorrow. He said he might go out to dinner with us, and that he felt a need to go to church.

I cooked hamburgers for dinner. That's what Otis wanted. Trey came. He stayed with Otis talking about the bible and praying with him. When Trey finished praying, Otis ate his burger. He ate very well. Trey left and went to church.

Otis got ready for bed. He seems to be doing all right. While he was sleeping, I observed his breathing. It was good. I noticed when he slept that he was breathing deeply. It seems to be easier. He may be in pain when he is awake though. He took more Tylenol today for that.

Frances called again. She talked and prayed. It was a blessing. I got up and prayed. I am still fasting for my husband's healing. I know God is able in the name of Jesus. The Lord has encouraged me so much doing this sickness.

June 11

I took Otis' vital signs.

Verna Mae called. She and her friend will stop by later. Otis ate his breakfast. Boo came by to do some work for us. While Boo was cutting the yard, Verna Mae and Melodye came by. Melodye had cancer and was healed. She ministered to Otis and prayed. The anointing was in this house. Vern told us about when Melodye was down sick and how the Lord had her to tell Melody that her sickness was not unto death. She then told Otis that the Lord was giving her that for Otis also.

When Vern called this morning asking about Otis, he told me he was fine. Usually, he says, "Okay," or "So, so." I thank God for working. While they were in the house ministering, Boo came in for a glass of water. He told me he was going back outside because he didn't want to listen to that. I told him one day he's going to wish for it.

Tricey came as Vern and Melodye were getting ready to leave. Otis told Tricey to come and give your daddy a hug. She was having problems with her car, so she went to have it looked at. Boo took Otis to the credit union. Otis told me to stay home and wait for Frank Fender's call. He was going to work on a refrigerator for us on Weare Street.

While Vern and Melodye were here, it came to me to tell them what happened before Otis got sick. *You know it is not good to mistreat God's children.* I spoke about how Otis had hurt me by not going to different functions with me and other things. In February, I had asked him to go someplace with me and he gave me an excuse. He had to do something for another lady at his church. I bet he did.

I was so hurt. I got out of bed, went to the front door, opened it and put my head out in the cold and told God I was tired. "I have had enough. I give him to you." I had been praying for him, and asking God for mercy, and to keep him safe.

It seems that on the night when I gave Otis back to God, the hedge was taken down and God allowed the enemy to start working. Otis got sick either the same or the next week. I told them, "When we pray, we don't know how God is going to work." Had I known Otis would get sick, I probably would not have prayed that way, but something good has come out of this. *Otis is saved, and we are closer.*

Tricey called to say it was going to take some time to fix her car and asked would I come get her. I told Miss Sister to get dressed, and I went to get Tricey.

We went to Sears to see more furniture. She did not like the set that I had picked out. She liked the set at Montgomery Ward a little.

I drove her back to get her car, and I came home. It cost more money to fix her car than what we had thought. Otis didn't want to go out to eat with us anymore, so I went and got him a fish dinner. Tricey came and we all—Mae, Miss Sister, Tricey and me—went to dinner. Otis still wanted to go to church so I was trying to rush with dinner, so we wouldn't be too late. Mae decided to have dessert, so we had to wait for her. She told Tricey not to rush her.

Tricey dropped me and Miss Sister off at home, so I could get my car and Otis. As we were getting in the car, Delores Woods came by. She talked to Otis for a while, and I wrote a check for Otis for their pastor's appreciation.

When we got to church, I took Miss Sister to the bathroom while they were praying. Otis went in while we were in the bathroom. The choir sang beautifully. Mary Easton led a song that said, "Hold on. Don't give up. There is someone who cares for you." Sheila Christie led a song that said, "Keep the faith," and Ray Whitley led a song that said, "Your labor will not be in vain." Glorious, Holy. Pastor got up and sang along with Ray in a song that said, "We need to hear from you."

When Pastor came up to preach, he came from 1 Timothy 2:1-4. Plus, Hebrews 3: John 17: and 1 Corinthians 6:12. As he spoke, the anointing was present. Afterward, he called for altar prayer. Otis went up. He stayed up there until he got tired. Mother Bright saw him and was so happy. While pastor was speaking, he mentioned some of the things Melodye had talked about and something Mother Bright had said. Pastor came out in the audience praying for people. Otis got in the aisle. Pastor prayed for him. He was on the floor. Minister Jones ministered to him. Tricey had come over and hugged him earlier.

Leron wanted to go up for prayer and I asked him if he wanted me to go with him. He said yes. We walked toward the front of the church. I saw Trey, so I told him Leron wanted prayer and I walked back to my seat. Trey talked to Leron and pastor went to the other side of the church. Leron stayed up front until pastor came back and prayed for him. He was on his knees on the floor. His mother, Anita went to get him up. He got up, and I saw tears in his eyes. I went over to him and hugged him. We stood there with our arms around each other's waist. I teased him about being ashamed for me to have my arms around him and he said he wasn't. I felt that he needed that support right then. I wanted him to know I care about him even though I'm not around much.

I started back to my seat. I felt it was time to get Otis home. Mother Bright stopped me and told me she thought it was about time for us to go. I asked Otis if he was ready to go and he said whenever I was ready. I went up front and got Miss Sister and brought her where we were, and I told Otis to come on. He told Miss Sister to sit down, so I stood up and praised God some more.

Pastor prayed for Ulysses, Frances' husband. He told him that if he would receive it, he would be a different person or man from this day forward. While pastor was praying for Ulysses, Frances was standing next to me hollering. That's what Ulysses been praying for, that Pastor would call him out. I couldn't hear what pastor was saying, she was so loud. I told her I don't know how you heard anything as loud as you are.

Church was over soon. Tony came over to give us a hug. He had been on the camera and playing his guitar. On our way out, I stopped by the tape room to speak to David, Larry, and Vasco. It had been a long time since I had been back there with them.

We got in the car and started home. Otis started coughing and spitting up. I started to pull over, but he told me to keep going. I had a chuck in the car, so it was able to hold all the vomit. He threw up almost all the way home. I know that was just the devil mad because he had gotten blessed and wanted to discourage him.

We got home and got ready for bed. I got my tea, read my bible and prayed.

June 12

Today was somewhat busy. I got up, prayed, took Otis' vital signs, and got his breakfast. He seems a little weaker.

Tricey and I went to look at furniture. She liked the set at Rhodes that Mae liked. We ended up getting it. It is to be delivered Thursday. While we were looking at the sofa, we asked Rick how it worked, and I know it was the Lord's doing because as soon as he opened out the bed I saw two holes in the mattress. He said he would mark it down thirty dollars. I told him, "That's ok. I don't want it." Then, he said,

"Wait. I think I can do something else." He left and came back and told me he would give me a full warranty on the sofa and that the manufacturer will send someone out with a new mattress. He said he will call them Monday and if I don't hear from them to give him a call.

Back home, Tricey got her clothes together and went over to Mae's to wash. Tony was at the house with his daddy. Otis told me that Fettie had called. Her daddy had surgery the day before and was doing fine.

As I sat in the living room reading the newspaper, I heard the tires of a car making a screeching sound, and then I heard a bam. I jumped up hoping it wasn't Tricey coming home. I saw a car across the street, and Stephanie, Willis from next door's girlfriend, came running across the street to the car. I called out to her to see if anyone was hurt not knowing it was her car.

When I got across the street, the car started moving toward the street, and she jumped in to stop it. I noticed the baby was in the backseat in his car seat asleep. She told me that she stopped the car, put it in park, ran to the mailbox, and the car started rolling. It rolled into the street. A car hit it on the passenger side, and it kept rolling until it got across the curb and sidewalk.

I thank God no other traffic was coming. This is a busy four-lane road. This was a blessing. I got the baby out of the car and put him on the sofa in the den. He didn't wake up. I was able to get in touch with Willie on his job, and he got here fast. The police came in and looked at the baby to make sure he was all right. He didn't wake up. They charged Stephanie with the accident.

Charles Myers, one of Otis' classmates came by. They sat and talked for a long time. Later Gene Timmons and Lawdy came by too. Lawdy was talking about cursing his mother-in-law out because she hadn't told him about Otis being sick. Trey and little Trey came by also. Lil Trey gave his granddaddy a hug and came and gave me one. Tony and DeAndrea and Adrienna came by also. Ms. A is getting so grown, she doesn't want me to hold her. I had to tell them to give granddaddy a hug. Debra Law and her daddy came by and sat with Otis for a long time earlier today.

Tricey left for Tallahassee about 5:00 pm.

Flammie, Rashad, Boo, and Debra came by just for a while. As they were leaving, Boo was talking to Otis. Otis was witnessing to Boo. Flammie was outside ready to go and started back in the house and I stopped her. I didn't want her to stop them.

Tricey made it back to Tallahassee okay. I went to the store to the store to pick up a few things and came back home. It was late, and I didn't feel like making potato salad. I cooked the potatoes and said I'll get up and fix it in the morning.

Otis wanted me to get his tithes added up. I got them added up and came back to tell him they were added including the ones I didn't give to my church because I felt he didn't want me to. I told him I could tell something was wrong with him when I told him I was going to give part to my church.

He went back to when I was working. I didn't do what I promised, and I spent more money than I put in and didn't do right by him. He said because of that, he shouldn't have to share his tithes from the property with me. He went on and on, and I told him that was in the past and we have to go on and stop talking about that every time we talk about money.

He forgot about the times I worked and paid all the bills but the house note, which was only 57.00 dollars a month. I had to pay the light and water bill, telephone, and the school bill for the boys. They were in private school. He seems to think I want to give the money to my church, so I can look good. I told him when I give, I give from my heart, and that I tithe off two dollars or whatever I have. He told me that God knows what I have, and he's not expecting any more from me than the tithes off the hundred I get from HRS.

He doesn't understand that it will be a blessing for him to allow me to give that little bit to my church. He says, why should he give to my church when his church needs it as much or more than mine. I don't think he can see what God wants him to do. I told him that I wouldn't ask him about splitting the tithes on the properties.

I got my tea, read my bible and went to bed at about three in the morning.

He had talked a long time.

June 13

I woke up at about nine, still tired and sleepy. I prayed and took Otis' vital signs.

~ His blood pressure is going up a little.

I got him breakfast. He is still eating just cereal. He didn't feel like going to church. I made the potato salad for Frances. I told Miss Sister we weren't going to church. Otis tried to get me to go, but I decided to stay home. He made a good point. He said he stays here when I go shopping, and he can stay now. He stayed in the bed most of the day. When he did get up, he said he felt fine, but he just didn't have any strength.

I started packing the things in the china cabinet. I didn't know it would take so long.

I got most of it done before I stopped to go get something to eat from Mae's house. She cooked greens, rice, chopped turkey drums, and baked sweet potatoes. I fixed three plates, came home, and warmed them up. Otis ate all but a small piece of potato. He said it was good and asked me to call Mae and tell her. I ate mine too. It was good. Miss Sister ate hers too.

Tina called to say hello. Ruby called. Deborah Hankerson and Deborah Wright called. While I was talking to Ruby, Trey called to pray with his daddy. After Trey prayed with him, Otis got up and walked outside. I called Mae and told her how good the food was. I talked to Eileen too.

After I finished cleaning in the kitchen, I made my tea and came in the bathroom to read and write in this book. It is getting late. I have to get up early to get Zak and Ms. Kailyn in the morning.

I didn't fast today. Tomorrow, I will be fasting for my husband's healing.

We decided to start back taking some of the medicine to see if he feels better.

One of our tenants (Shirley) called. She was complaining about the refrigerator not working even though the man had been there to work on it. She said she has decided to move when her lease is up. I told her we would not have a problem with her moving. She says the house just has too many problems.

I am going to say my prayers and go to bed.

Tricey called tonight to tell me that Sid graduated from high school Friday. I told her I happy for him.

Earlier tonight, as I was standing in the kitchen, it was impressed upon me to tell Otis to tell God he was sorrow and to say it from his heart. I wondered if it was me talking, and I started praying and scripture came to my mind. "It is not you that speaks, but the Lord," found in Matthew.

I felt as if Otis was contending with God because he was talking as if he didn't owe me anything since I quit my job and I know God told me to. He came in the kitchen and I told him what was impressed upon me to tell him. "Tell God you are sorry from your heart and ask Him to tell you what that is about." I was not going to tell Otis what I thought it was about. The last time he came up against me about having to pay for my nursing license, he got sick and had to go into the hospital. I don't want that to happen. Otis needs to be taught the ways of the Lord, but he will not listen to me.

I know when God forgives, you are forgiven, and it is gone unless you do it again.

June 14

I was awakened at 6:30 am. It was Fred bringing Zak. I turned the TV on for him and laid back down. I wanted to get another thirty minutes before Ms. Kailyn got here. She came at 7:00 am. Trey came in and gave me a hug. Tony called right after to say Deborah was on her way to get Zak to drop him off at ABC for camp.

I gave Kailyn her bath, dressed her and fed her. She was ready for her cream of wheat and eggs. Miss Sister wanted grits. I gave them to her. Otis wanted cereal, so I prepared that for him. He ate it. Kailyn tried her best to get some of the cereal out of the bowl.

I had taken Otis' vital signs earlier. I sat on the side of the bed and Otis told me he was sorry. I asked, "What are you sorry for?" He said, "I said I am sorry if I hurt you." *If* is a big word. I think he was reaching out to me. I told him I was sorry too. He said he was sorry if he wronged me not if he hurt me. Then I said, "I am sorry because I probably did you wrong without knowing."

He said he felt weak, so he was in the bed during the morning until his coworker, Harold Lawton came by. Otis came up front and talked to him for a while. He ate watermelon and a sausage sandwich and drank Gatorade.

It was time to feed Kailyn. I gave her her food and wiped her off and told her it was time for a nap. She got in my lap and went to sleep. She slept a long time—about three hours.

Earlier, Kailyn, Miss Sister and I went to Raines High School to get Andy. The bus didn't pick her up. I carried her to FCCJ North Campus. Then, I went to Walmart.

Edmond Peterson came to see Otis. They sat in the living room and talked for a long time. Edmond went to the car and brought a photo album back. They looked in the album and discussed who was who. I left to drop Kailyn over to Mama Collins. I had to meet someone on the east side.

When I came back, Baby Sister was here. She left after I got home.

I went to get one of my gas tablets and saw the box open. I asked Otis if he had to get something for gas and he told me Baby Sister did. I told him that they have something about not closing things up. He said I guess so.

I went to Mae's to get some greens. I stopped by Popeyes to get some chicken. I got home and fixed him a plate. I had made potato salad yesterday.

~ He ate well.

After we finished eating, I went to get the water and clothes out of the washing machine. It took me about thirty minutes. I decided to test the machine again. I placed it on the cycle just for rinse, and I came back to the bedroom to tell him it was spinning. When I got back in the utility room, water was going in the machine. I turned it to the spin cycle, the water would not go out, I had to dip it out again.

When I finish with the water, I thought about the insurance forms that I needed to take to the doctor tomorrow. I filled them out and placed them in my purse.

It is late. Again, Otis is still coughing. He has been coughing off and on all day. Sometimes, he coughs up blood.

We decided to start back taking some of the pills today. Tonight, we started on the breathing pills again. Later in the night, I asked if he was breathing better. He said, "I think so." Later, I asked if he was spitting up more. He said, "Yes, mucus but not blood."

Melodye called today, the young lady that came by Friday with Vern. She told me to tell him she is praying for him and that she called. I forgot to tell him. I hope I remember when I go into the room. Sister Givens called too. She wanted to know how he was doing, and she told me she was going to get a book about healing for him to read from gospel world.

I have had my tea for tonight, so I think I'll say my prayers and go to bed. Today was Mama's (Varnadore) birthday. She is 79 years old. They had ice cream and cake, but Otis didn't feel strong enough to go over.

I forgot to write last month, around the 28th, that I believe I heard the Lord say He is healing Otis, but it was something He had to work out in him first.

June 15

I got up early to let Zak in. I ask him if he could tell time. He said yes. I told him to wake me at 7:15 am. I was so tired and sleepy. At 7:15 am Zak came in the room and touched me. I got up, slipped on some clothes, and went to take him to ABC for camp. I didn't know I had to go in to sign him in.

I got back home, took Otis' vitals, prepared his breakfast and got dressed for the doctor's office.

~ Otis is still weak.

He had to have blood work done before going to Dr. Luke's office. I put him out at the door and drove around looking for a parking place. All the handicapped spaces were taken. I found one, parked and went upstairs to the doctor's office to ask if they could order blood gases drawn because he was really tired and weak.

I felt that he wasn't getting enough oxygen. Dr. Luke told me we would have to go over to the hospital to have that done because they couldn't do them in the lab downstairs. I went down to the lab and gave Otis' papers to the girl at the desk. We didn't have to wait long before they called him in the back. They were busier than usual. Upstairs in Dr. Luke's office, they weighed him. 182 and 1/2 pounds. He had gained weight for a change.

Dr. Luke stated he wants to wait two more weeks before Otis starts any new treatment. He called for the oxygen, and we went to the hospital to have the blood gases drawn. Dr. Luke told us that he was going to write off the twenty percent that the insurance doesn't pay. We told him thanks. We thanked the Lord too. As a matter of fact, Otis said thanked the Lord while I was telling the doctor thanks.

At the hospital, I signed him in and sat down. I heard Otis Wright being called and I got up to go to the desk thinking it sure didn't take long. However, it was a phone call from Dr. Luke's office. Gladys was calling to tell us we didn't need to have the blood drawn because our insurance didn't require it before they paid.

We left the hospital. We went by mama's. He wanted to see her. We stayed there a long time. I kept thinking about all the work I had to do at home. When we left, he wanted to go find a watermelon. The people weren't on the corner. He wanted to go to the farmer's market. I was saying to myself, "Why today?" We rode around the market until he saw a watermelon. Then, he wanted mangoes and peaches.

We finally got home. He had company, a coworker named Henderson. The people came with the oxygen and showed us how to use it. We also had a portable tank to carry out if we have to go out.

Baby Sister, came while they were hooking up the oxygen. She got upset. She left. Later, I discovered she called Pop to tell him about oxygen. He called to see what was going on.

At Mama's house, there was a banner that said happy birthday from all her children. I had all their names printed on it. I looked for the one we had signed, but I didn't see it. I felt maybe they didn't want me to sign it, so they made another one. I felt a little hurt that I wasn't included after being in the family for thirty-one years.

The oxygen seemed to help. Otis sat up front with it on for a long time.

Otis had more company. Mr. H., a classmate of his, stopped by.

He prayed for Otis and Miss Sister. During his prayer, I felt that it wasn't quite sincere. I didn't say anything. I said I was probably wrong, but later, Otis said he didn't think Mr. H. was quite right, but he didn't want to judge him.

After transferring the oxygen to the bedroom, we got ready for bed. It was late.

June 16

I was awakened by Zak coming in. I was so tired. I wanted to lay down, but I had too much I had too much to do. I called Eileen. She told me she was going to pick Waltina up because she was stranded on Kings Road. I told her that I was going that way to take Zak to ABC, and I will pick her up.

I prayed before I left home. I dropped Zak off and picked Waltina up. Back home, I started trying to put things in boxes. Eileen and Brittany came over. We got lots of boxes filled and moved into Tricey's room and Miss Sister's room.

The man came to lay the carpet. Eileen and Waltina helped him get a lot of furniture out before his help came. Eileen and Waltina worked really hard, even though Tina wasn't feeling well. Eileen carried Tina home and came back. She worked until almost three. She left to go get her Mother. She came back and worked some more. I know I am going to do something nice for her and Tina. I did the vacuuming after they laid it down.

I think they were trying to take advantage of us.

Eileen left to go work with the witnessing team at church. She is so faithful in the ministry.

The carpet was finally finished at about 8:00 pm. All of the furniture was back in the house. It really looks good.

This is the night Mr. H. came by. As you can see, I have gotten behind again, and I have forgotten how things went. Anyway, I left Miss Sister here with Otis and I went to get us something to eat. He ate well, watched TV. He went to bed.

I tried to do a little more work before I got my tea and came in the bathroom to read my bible.

Sister Givens came by today and brought a little book for Otis to read. She had prayer with us. Also, Reverend Calhoun came by and brought two cantaloupes and a watermelon.

Before they could get the old carpet and padding up and on the trash pile good, someone came by to ask for the padding. Otis says she has a little place where she sells stuff.

Also, Clarence Yates came by. He sat in the den with Otis for a good while. He was telling Otis about his son Alan. Otis told him to tell Alan to come and get that old car of Trey's, and he can have it. I had told him the other day, not to sell it, but give it away and the Lord will bless him.

June 17

I awoke because Zak was at the door. I took him to ABC.

I got back home and waited for the furniture for the den. Willie Scott called to say he couldn't get the old furniture because he didn't have any place to store it. The furniture came.

I had already taken Otis' vital signs and gave him his breakfast as I do every morning.

When they got the sofa in, they wanted me to sign that it was in good condition. I told them about the tear in the mattress, and they told me I was supposed to get it as is. I told them that I was given a full warranty on it because of the tear and it is to be replaced. He then got another slip for me to sign stating it was damaged. I still signed the other slip.

Otis came in the den to see the furniture. He liked it. He sat down and stayed there. Miss Sister came in and sat with him. I got his oxygen and plugged it in. He laid down on the sofa and when to sleep. He stayed there all day. So did I.

Tony and the girls came by to see the furniture. Deborah had stopped by earlier.

Tony hooked the phone up in the sofa for me and he fixed the VCR hook up for me. I ate my leftovers. Otis ate something else.

He is still having that nagging pain in the lower part of his back. He takes Tylenol for pain. He went outside and walked down the street. He came back saying he started aching. I got a sheet and placed it over his legs. I should have thought about that earlier. I think it might be the air conditioner, blowing cold air on him.

Tony and the girls left. Otis got ready for bed. I was in the kitchen when came up behind me and told me he needed me to do something for him. I told him I will be back there as soon as I finish, and he told me not to take all night.

We watched TV together before going to bed. I guess he just wanted me to be in the room with him.

I am just plain old tired. I feel exhausted.

I read my bible and prayed before going to sleep.

Trey called and prayed with him earlier.

June 18

Zak came. He went into the den to watch TV, and I went back to sleep. I told him to wake me at 7:15 am. I woke up as he was coming to get me.

I prayed. I thanked God for his goodness. I thanked him for saving Otis. I asked him to sanctify the fast as I fast for his healing. I believe he is healed. His body just has to regain its strength.

I carried Zak to ABC, signed him in and came home. I took Otis' vital signs and gave him his breakfast and tried to get him to get up and get dressed. We needed to go to the State Board of Health. He told me we would have to go at another time because he felt weak. I got the oil and prayed for him and told to get up. He said he will later, but he wanted to lay there right now. I told him he had to give God something to work with. He had to believe what we prayed and act on it. He got up and went into the den and got on the sofa. There, he stayed all day.

Looking back, I can see now that I wanted to believe he was healed. I wouldn't let myself think that I was losing my husband.

I went to the bank to make a deposit and to the grocery store to pick up a few things. I picked up some fried fish that he wanted for lunch and I fixed Miss Sister and me a sausage sandwich. He read his bible and the commentary for a while. Then, he looked at TV.

Trey came by. He likes the furniture and carpet. He prayed with Otis before he left.

Tricey told me she was coming home this morning. I began to get concerned when she had not arrived by two o'clock. I called the house, but I didn't get an answer. Later, I talked to Sheila and she told me she left about eleven or eleven thirty. It was about four o'clock now. I didn't know if something had happened or not. I couldn't go out to dinner not knowing.

I left to go out east. I stopped to get Mae and saw Tricey's car before I got to the house. I had prayed on my way over. She was in there on the phone. She says she didn't leave Tallahassee until late.

Mae and I went out east and back to get Miss Sister and Tricey. Flammie came by earlier, she liked the carpet and sofa.

We went to Cedar River to eat. We wanted seafood. It was good.

Bay and Josh came by while Flammie was here.

Bay got to talking about she is a Christian. Trey asked her what a Christian is. She said it is someone who believes in God. Trey told her it means Christ-like. She wanted to know what Christ was like. He told her it is in the bible how he went about doing good and being an example for the people by loving and caring for people.

Trey asked Flammie if she died, where would she spend eternity. She said she wasn't worried about that. She was just trying to be happy from day to day and God knows. She and Flammie left. Flammie was uncomfortable too, as they were talking.

Flammie and Patsy came and brought Otis some fried fish and salad. He ate some of it. He sat on the sofa in the den looking at the baseball and basketball games on TV.

Addie Blount called. I saw her at the service station and told her about Otis being sick and that they say it is cancer. She told me they told her she had terminal cancer a long time ago, but she never went to the hospital. God healed her. Anyway, tonight when she called, she got both of us on the phone. She talked and told us that she had been in prayer about Otis' situation and the Lord told her he was already healed. Halleluiah. She told us how the Lord told her that if she had the surgery she would die because the doctors wouldn't know what to do, it was so bad.

She said her family was upset and panicking, but she trusted the Lord. She told us to read the healing scriptures and minister to ourselves through the word of God. She also quoted some scriptures to him from Isaiah 53. She said the Lord told her it is well with Otis. She told him to walk in the victory. She also prayed for his lungs, voice and body organs, muscles and back pain, and leg pain. She prayed for my strength too. She also said that Otis can't go yet because God is not through with him. He is going to be a testimony for the Lord.

It is late now, so I am going to bed.

Thank you Lord for this day. Help me to sleep in the spirit and wake in the spirit, ready to work for you, in Jesus' name. Bless our sleep, especially Otis'. Lord, I thank you. Bless us to have a blessed and fruitful day tomorrow, in Jesus' name, Amen.

Addie also told Otis when he requests more tests, they won't be able to find any cancer. Walk in victory. It's already done.

June 19

I woke up late, prayed, and took Otis vital signs. His respiration is fast, like he is short of breath. I don't understand that. He still has the oxygen going.

He said he feels better today. I made breakfast, waffles with syrup and sausage. He didn't want it, but he did try to eat it.

Deborah dropped DeAndrea and Adrienne off. Adrienne came in the room while Otis was eating and wanted some of the food. Otis said, "Thank God I have someone to help me eat."

He went in the living room to sit down to read the newspaper. Before he came out of the room, he was starting to feel bad again from that pain in the back.

He asked me had I told Addie about the pain in his crouch. I told him no because I didn't know about it. When she prayed, she kept praying for the discomfort in the pelvic area. I prayed with him and told him he had to get up even if he didn't feel like it. He had to resist the devil. Give God something to work with.

Earlier, the doorbell rang, and he was up and at the door before I could move. Telling me, "I'll get it." Then, that devil attacked him again. I know I have to keep talking faith to him.

Tricey and I were sitting in the den watching TV and Otis started complaining about all the boxes that had to be emptied. We had to put things back in place. I told him I was going to do it. I got up from the sofa and went into my bedroom to clean up or at least make the bed.

I dressed and told him I was going to wash clothes and go to the east side. Miss Sister rode with me. I washed one load and placed them in the dryer. I washed another load, and I didn't like the way they smelled, so I washed them again. After the second load finished washing, I came home and put them in the dryer.

I got Otis some dinner. He ate it pretty good, so did Miss Sister and I. Otis ate watermelon and cantaloupe earlier.

I start putting the glasses in the china cabinet. After I clean the glass, I realized the glasses insider were dirty. I am going to wash them, but not tonight. I put the books in the bookcase. I think I have gotten most of them in.

Tricey went over to Mae's to wash her clothes. She came back and started making phone calls. She finally got in touch with Twyla. They decided to go off. I told her it was not fair that she didn't want to help me by even washing the dishes.

She says that she told me to throw the books away. I told her I was not going to throw my books away. She got a shower and got dressed. Twyla came, and they left after Tricey asked me to kiss her good night. I told her don't even try it. I was getting angry and wanted her to leave me alone. I let her kiss my forehead, so she would go. She left saying, "I'll be back after a while."

I called my brother Leroy to see if he was coming to the family reunion. He said he will be there. He is going to fly. Then, I called my brother Mack. He talked as if he might come. His wife Clara was all for it. I told her to push him into coming.

Otis has that pain in the lower part of his back again. He wants Tylenol. I get it for him.

Now, I am going to read my bible and pray before going to bed.

June 20

I was awakened by the phone. It was Frances calling. We talked briefly, and I went back sleep.

I woke earlier to see the TV broadcast. I only saw a portion of it. When it went off, I asked Otis to change the station so I can see Rodney's broadcast. I only saw part of that. I was sleepy.

I got up so I could take Otis' vital signs. His breathing is still fast. His says he feels pretty good. I made breakfast for him. He ate most of it. I made sausage and waffles.

Tricey came into the room with gifts for Otis. This is Father's Day. He read the cards from Trey, Lil Trey, Cynthia and Kailyn and Tricey. He started crying. I thought at first something was wrong with him. I started asking, "What's wrong?" He said, "I'm all right." Then, I knew it was the cards. I knew what Tricey's card said because I read it. It was touching. So was Trey's. Otis said, "I love you all so much," and I said, "We love you too."

By now, Tricey has tears in her eyes, and so did I. He was trying to open his gifts and Tricey asked if he wanted her to help him. He got most of the wrapping off and she pulled the other part off. She had bought him a beautiful pair of blue shorts with a striped shirt to match. She had also picked out a gift for me for him, a pair of green shorts, with a shirt to match. I think he liked his gifts.

I went down to New Bethlehem Baptist Church to take his tithes. I prayed on my way over that I will see someone I know outside the building. As soon as I parked the car, I saw Deacon Ronald Thompson. I hurried around there before I could lose him. He was standing up talking to Deacon Irving Eddy. When Deacon Eddy saw me, I saw his expression changed. I knew he was probably thinking I was coming to tell them that Otis was dead.

I was smiling and speaking as I approached them. Deacon Eddy asked, "Are you all right?" I said, "Yes, thank God." Again, he said, "Are you all right?" I told him I was fine. Then, he asked, "How's Deac?" I told them he is fair. He has good days and bad. I told them I had come to bring his tithes. That's when Deacon Eddy changed his expression. I talked a little more and left.

I stopped by the store to pick up a few things before going home.

Tricey and I unwrapped the dishes. I placed them in the china cabinet and I placed some of the glasses in also. I couldn't put all of them in since they needed to be washed. Tricey and I argued because she wants to throw out things that I wanted to keep.

I stopped and cooked. I made chicken with cream of mushroom and celery soup, and I cooked rice with herb for our cream of mushroom and celery soup. I made speckled butter beans for a vegetable. It tasted okay.

Tony came by on his way to work and dropped off a gift for his daddy and gave him a hug. He gave him a pajama set. It was a nice knee length set that was gray and trimmed in maroon. Otis was happy.

Trey and Cynthia came by to bring Miss Sister home from church. They told me about service being rally day. Different people were pledging money for the renovation of the church. Cyn told me Trey pledged two thousand dollars for his daddy's healing. They visited with us for a while. I asked them if they wanted to eat. Cyn told me she was taking Trey out to dinner for Father's Day. Kailyn was hungry. She got up to the table and pointed at the bread. I asked Cyn if she could have a piece. She said, "Yes, my baby is probably hungry because she hasn't eaten any lunch." I took a slice of bread and tore it in half and gave it to her. She ate it and reached for the other piece. They left.

Tricey left for Tallahassee at about four o'clock. The young fellow that was to ride with her came here at about four twenty. I told him she was gone. She had been to his house and called me from a neighbor to see if he had called. He said he didn't have another ride and left. He called back to see if she had come back by here.

Deborah and the girls came by to see Otis for Father's Day. They looked pretty with their white and purple on. Kailyn had on navy blue and white. She looked pretty too.

I fed Miss Sister. Margaret and Pop walked over here to see Otis. Otis witnessed to Pop about tithing and read some scripture from the bible to him. Pop did not want to hear it, but I think he listened. Pop helped a man outside with his stalled car. The young lady came in to get some cold water. Pop and Margaret left.

Frances, Ulysses and Tony C. came by. Ulysses came in asking for something to eat. I fixed Otis' plate. I gave Ulysses and Tony C something to drink, and I gave Ulysses a piece of chicken and bread. Tony didn't want anything. Frances fixed herself something too.

Gail and Judy came by also. They admired my new carpet and sofa. They told me about service too. They talked, and I said let me call Pastor now to make my pledge. I talked to Sister Callahan and told her I just wanted to let them know that I am with them, and I am pledging three hundred or more. She thanked me and asked about Otis.

Tricey called to let us know she made it back.

Cecil came just as Frances, Gail, and the others were leaving. They liked Cecil's car. I told them that's what I want. Cecil stayed and talked to Otis for quite some time. I didn't go in the den. I let them have that time alone. I know Otis enjoyed his company.

I finished cleaning up in the kitchen and took the trash and the recycle things. I had cut up three cantaloupes that were going bad. They were not sweet.

Otis came to the room to lay down. I brought the oxygen back here and turned it on just in case he wanted it.

Now, I'm writing in this tablet and reading my bible. I keep thinking about my son Tony. Why is he so negative about the church? Does he know he is cutting his blessing? *(In hindsight, I now know.)* I know I need to talk to him and I pray God gives me wisdom how. I believe he has held up his blessings on his job. That's why he is having problems on the job. All I can say right now is Lord have mercy on him. I have finished writing for tonight. Now, it is time to read.

June 21

It is about 6:30 am. Deborah Hankerson is calling to say Fred and Zak are on the way.

I laid there for a few more minutes. I got up, walked up front, and looked around. I turned on the TV in the den and sat down. The doorbell rings. I let Zak in and tell them that Cynthia is going to take Zak today.

Zak goes into the den to look at TV. I go back to bed for about twenty minutes. I get up, pray, and go up front. The doorbell rings.

Cyn and Kailyn are here. I am still sleepy. Kailyn looks sleepy too. Cyn says she might go back to sleep because she just picked her up from her bed and brought her over here. Cyn and Zak leave for camp and work.

Kailyn and I get in the bed with Otis. He is not feeling well. His legs and backache. He has been taking Tylenol.

I wake up, get on my knees to pray, and I thank God for the fast, as I fast for my husband's healing.

I thank God for healing him.

Kailyn wakes up. I give her a bath and me. I take Otis' vital signs. His respiration is not fast today. Thank God. He wants cereal for breakfast. I get it for him and I have Kailyn's cream of wheat cooling. She tries to eat his cereal and he gives it to her. I told her to come eat her breakfast, but she didn't want to leave his. I finally get her to the kitchen. She eats all of her breakfast. Miss Sister wanted grits. I get it for her.

We all came into the den. We watched TV. Kailyn played and got into other things. She and I went for a short walk. She was kind of sleepy. I didn't want her to go to sleep until she ate her lunch. She ate all of her lunch. She pooped in her diaper. As I was changing her, she went to sleep. I fixed my lunch and went in the bedroom to eat and TV. I didn't want to disturb Otis or have him fussing about what I was eating.

Wouldn't you know it? He came back here and asked if there were any more fried chicken. I finished eating and got it for him.

Bartley came by. I told him I thought they were gone. He said they will leave tomorrow. They are going on a trip that Otis and I were planning to go on. I guess it wasn't God's will. He and Otis talked for a long time. Kailyn woke up and tried to play with him. When he left, Otis and I told him to have a nice and safe trip, and tell everyone hello.

Otis is still having pain in his leg and back. I gave him a pill. I keep talking to him, telling him to rebuke the pains in the name of Jesus. He repeats what I say, but I tell him it had to come from the heart.

When I look back, I can feel the fear in both of us.
Me hoping he will be healed. Him afraid he was going to die.
I was in denial.

Cyn came to get Kailyn. She told us she is a surplus teacher and may not be working. She was concerned because Trey had made a pledge to the church. I told her that God will work it out.

Nathaniel Jackson came by to see Otis. They sat in the den and talked for a long time. Also, the old man that wanted to get an apartment from the eastside came by to bring the papers for me to fill out. They all left.

I got Miss Sister and my dinner. When we finished, I went to Pic and Sav to get some Tylenol. I got back and went in the kitchen to wash the glasses, so I could put them back in the china cabinet.

Earlier, Annette Bell called to see how Otis was doing and to see if he was ready for a class reunion here at the house. He told me no and for them to go on with their plans and let him know what happens. He told me they wanted to have a meeting here, and he didn't want that. He thinks I wouldn't clean up good enough. Annette asked me about coming to the meeting in his place. I told her I will have to let her know.

Barbara Jean called also to see how Otis was doing. Another classmate came by named Michael. He sat with Otis and talked for some time.

At eight o'clock, Otis and I watched the TV broadcast. I was so comfortable on the sofa, I went to sleep. I would wake up at intervals. I know my body is tired, I thought I could stay awake to see the broadcast, especially after I have not been to church for a while. I know it was the enemy putting me to sleep. It happened so fast I didn't have time to rebuke it in Jesus' name.

Katina called to see how Otis was doing and to talk.

It is late, so I am going to try to read, and go to bed.

June 22

I got up to let Zak in and laid down again. I told Zak to wake me up at 7:15.

I was just getting into the sleep when I felt someone touch me. It was Zak standing by the bed. I looked at the clock and said, "It's seven o'clock." He didn't want to be late because they are going on a field trip. I got up.

I went into the bedroom to clean up. My mind told me that Zak was going to the door. I didn't close the door. I was standing there naked when I turned around and glimpsed a blue shirt going. I said, "What are you doing in here?" He didn't answer. He was gone. When I got dressed, I went up front and told him, "You couldn't wait on me. You had to see what I was doing." He just looked at me and laughed.

I took him to camp.

Otis got up to walk and told me got tired. His legs felt like they were going to give out on him. He says they are still aching. I took his vital signs. I asked him what he wants for breakfast. He said cereal. I got it for him. He ate and took his medication. He asked me to call Dr. Luke to see if he could increase his oxygen and Lasix[13]. He stayed in bed most of the day.

I tried to put some of the things away out of the boxes. I had to go to the bank, the insurance office, and the grocery store. Otis wanted some canned beef stew. I got home and fixed him a can of the stew. He ate it all. I fixed my lunch and asked Miss Sister if she was hungry. She said no. She was still full from the cereal this morning.

As I was eating, Sister Peoples called. We talked for about two hours about the goodness of the Lord and my husband's healing. She began telling me she could feel the anointing all over my house. As she said it, I felt the anointing on me. I thank God for being so good to me. She also told me about oiling my body with anointed oil after showering. I got off the phone to do something for Otis and to fix Miss Sister something to eat. Otis is the one that got the oil on his body.

As I sat looking at the TV, I started thinking back on Otis' sickness. I felt that in six months, he was going to be well. It's not long

---

[13] A prescription medicine used to prevent fluid retention in the body

now before those six months will be up. I just have to keep thanking God for his healing and have a closer walk with the Lord. I have to keep encouraging Otis. He came up front when Clarence came to pick up the Fairmont[14]. It looks funny out there with the car gone. It has been out there so long. He gave the car to Clarence's son.

I started trying to straighten up again. I don't know where all this stuff is going.

I fixed Miss Sister and me some leftovers. Otis didn't want that, so I went to Mom's Kitchen and got him an oxtail dinner. He only ate a small amount.

I sat down on the sofa with Otis. We talked. I told him to just thank God for his healing even when there is pain. I told him since he knows he is healed, he doesn't have to worry about dying. Just thank God for the healing. He told me he wants to live, but he's not afraid of dying. He said he stopped being afraid a long time ago.

I think I was more afraid of him dying than he was. I just couldn't think of him leaving me.

When I look back, I was being selfish, knowing he was in pain.

I know God knows what he is doing, even if we don't see it or understand it.

I talked to both of my daughters-in-law. Cyn says she is working as of today. I told her all things work together for the good.

I know God knows what he is doing, even if we don't see it or understand it.

Otis and I were looking over our bank slip which shows what was left in the account. He talked about what was outstanding and mailed checks. He told me to write a check for the L. C. Callahan TV Ministry. I see God is doing a work.

Well, I am going to be obedient to what Sister Peoples said. I am going to take a shower and oil my body with anointed oil. The song, "Glory Halleluiah, Look What God is Doing," keeps coming to my mind. I know God is working for me and for my husband.

As I look back, I see where God has brought him from.

---

[14] A car made by Ford Motor in the late 1970s

I thank God for saving him.

It is late. My body is clean and oiled. It feels good. I oiled him too, his head, back, and legs. It's time now for reading my bible, praying, drinking my tea and going to bed.

~   Otis is coughing a lot. He is bringing up mucus.

While I was taking my shower, I heard him talking and thought he was talking to me. I asked him what did he say and he said, "I was talking to the Lord."

June 23

Today started like most days. I first got a call from Deborah to say Zak and Fred were on the way. I got up to cut the TV on in the den. I go to the door and wait for them.

When they come, I opened the door and waved at Fred. Zak goes into the den.

I lay down for a few minutes. I got up, slipped on some clothes over my PJs, and I took Zak to camp at ABC.

Back home, I laid down again and went to sleep.

I woke up at about 9:00 am. I got me a cup of coffee and came in the bathroom. I told Otis last night that we had to get up early, get a bath and get dressed because this is the day that Reverend Calhoun usually comes to see him.

Well, while I was in the bathroom, the doorbell rang. It was Thelma W. Otis' classmate's wife. She came in and sat and talked with us for a long time. I still had my PJs on. Otis had on a pair of shorts.

As we were talking, Tricey called. When I told her we had company, she said, "People don't know not to visit before 12 noon?" I just laughed. It really doesn't matter sometimes, especially if you know the people are concerned about you.

Tricey talked to her daddy as Thelma and I talked some more. Otis came back into the living room and sat down. We were talking when I looked toward the window in the den and saw Reverend Calhoun's truck turn into the yard. I jumped up, told Thelma that Otis' pastor was coming, and I had to put on some clothes. I asked will she open the door for me.

When I came back in the living room, Otis told me, "She opened the door for Reverend Calhoun and left." Reverend Calhoun said, "I must have run her away." He stayed and talked with Otis for a brief time. He prayed and left.

I took Otis' vital signs and gave him a little cereal. He ate it well. He stayed in the room most of the day. I made sausage dogs for Miss Sister and me. It was good.

I sat and looked at TV. Mazella came by later in the day. We looked through some cookbooks. Otis wanted some beans and wieners, so I fixed that for him. He ate that pretty good. Mae left to go to the store.

I asked Otis what he wants from the store so I could go there and get back to the house. He wanted pork chops, fruit and a different kind of cereal than what he has been eating. I picked up everything he wanted and cereal for Miss Sister. Also, I picked up ingredients for a cake. I decided to bake one for Otis. Our anniversary is tomorrow.

I got home, cooked the pork chops and opened a can of green beans. I fixed Miss Sister's plate when I finished cooking. Otis wasn't ready to eat. Tony came as I was cooking. He went in the bedroom with his daddy. I asked Otis if he was ready to eat and he said no. I asked Tony and he said no. As I was talking to Otis, Tony went up front. When I got to the kitchen, I saw him with a piece of pork chop on a paper towel. I gave him a plate because he was about to put barbecue sauce on it. He looked at me as I walked in and said, "You caught me." When he finished eating, I asked if it was good. He said, "Yes, but I won't eat another one."

I fixed my plate and sat down to eat. I looked around and Tony had two slices of bread and another pork chop with barbecue sauce on it.

I am glad he wasn't hungry. I would not have had enough to feed him.

Deborah and the girls came by. They had been to McDonald's. They were excited. They asked if they could have a piece of pork chop too. After I gave Otis his dinner, I gave them a plate too. They sat on the floor to eat. Otis ate all of his dinner. I thank God for that. Deborah ended up eating the rest of A's pork chop. Tony had a big bowl of ice cream and came back for more. The girls had ice cream too.

Frances called to tell me someone had broken into their apartment and taken a few things. Trey called so I had to get off the phone with Frances, so Trey could talk to his daddy.

I baked the cake. It looks good. I sure hope it tastes good. I was experimenting.

I was looking for Otis' prayer handkerchief that Pastor Callahan had sent him, and I found a gift in his closet. I didn't say anything. I just acted as if I didn't see it.

I don't have a gift for him. It hasn't come back yet. I feel bad because I don't have anything. I asked him to tell me something he wanted that I could get for him and he said he couldn't think of anything. I kept asking him to tell me something and he said, "You can't give me what I want—my health."

With tears in my heart, because I didn't want him to see me crying, I looked at him and told him I can tell someone else to give it to him (God). Then he said, "We always take health for granted until it is gone." I looked at him and told him, "It's not gone. It may have diminished, but it's not gone." He looked and said, "Thanks. I needed that."

I am trying to keep him encouraged.

I told him I wish I could give him a new me. He said, "No. I like this one." I said, "I mean losing weight." He said, "Don't worry about it." I told him that God was going to help me lose, and he said, "I hope it's not like this by being sick." I told him that God has already told me I wouldn't be sick, but I am going to lose.

I told Otis that I am eating more. I told him I see that he can't eat, and I think I am trying to eat for him. He looked at me and nodded his head. Here it is 22 years later, and I am losing weight. I am not trying to. It's just happening. I forgot what God said until I started writing this book.

I took the cake out of the oven, made my tea, went to my office (bathroom) to write in this tablet and read my bible. Then, I go to bed. Otis still has the oxygen going. He seems to be more dependent on it. He is still weak, and he still has that nagging pain in the lower part of his back and leg. I am still thanking God for his healing. I know it's there. Thinking back, my mind and my heart were close to what was going on. Denial to what is happening before me.

June 24

It's 1:00 am.

As I was praying for my husband, I asked the Lord to show us what to do. He told me to wait on Him. I thank God for allowing me to hear him. Thank you, Lord.

This is our 31st wedding anniversary. It doesn't seem like it's been that long. Thank God we have some good memories. We are blessed to have three wonderful children and four beautiful grandchildren. Trey and Cynthia have Trey, Edward, and Kailyn. LeAnthony and Deborah have DeAndrea, the oldest of all our grands, and Adrienna. Carolyn, our daughter, is a senior at Florida State University.

Zak came. I took him to camp after I prayed.

Back home, I took Otis' vital signs when he woke up. He says he feels pretty good. He ate a little raisin bran cereal this morning. Around noon, Otis wanted peaches and mango fruit. I gave it to him. He sat the living room briefly to eat the fruit and read the paper.

Cecil came by to see him. Miss Sister and I ate a sausage dog. I watched TV and nodded off to sleep. I am still trying to get things in order. I don't know where I am going to put all these boxes of stuff.

I asked Otis what he wanted for dinner. He said he wanted barbecue from Jenkins. I asked him if that is what he really wanted. He said he really wanted to take me out for dinner, but he didn't feel like going. He said he wanted steak. I told him I will cook it for him. He said no. He wants to get it from Quincey's if they have takeout. I told him I didn't know about Quincey's, but I know Ryan's has takeout. He told me to go get it and get what I wanted and what Miss Sister wants since I was going to get food. I asked her if she wanted what was already in there. She said she wanted what's in there. I think she thought she would have to pay for it. I decided to fix her dinner for her before I left.

I went to the east side to see a tenant. Then, I went Ryan's. Back home, I placed a tablecloth on the table, put candles in the crystal candle holders that Bob and Angie gave me for Mother's Day. I took out the china and glasses and set the table.

I went to get Otis. He was lying in the bed. He said, "I thought you weren't going to come see about your husband." I told him I was getting the table ready. He didn't want to, but he came to the table so he could eat. He looked at the setup and said, "You have everything so pretty." He ate almost half of his steak, half of the potato, a little of the tossed salad, and part of the dinner roll. I also made sweet tea to pour over ice. It was good.

I talked to Johnnie K., Flammie, Mae, Baby Sister and Tricey. Then, I gave Otis a piece of the cake I made last night, and I ate a piece myself.

Otis had Tricey to pick up a gift for me. She bought a beautiful purple short set. It was a bit big, so I will have to take it back. Also, Tricey had picked a beautiful card for her daddy and sent it to me. She also sent us a card. She is so sweet sometimes. Tricey called tonight to see how our anniversary was going.

I had not rented a car for next weekend. It took some time calling around to get the prices. I reserved several cars for me and Mae.

It seems that Otis is getting too dependent on that oxygen. He stays in the room now with it on all day. I told him he has to do something in order to gain his strength. I want to decrease it without him knowing.

Now, I know how bad that would have been.
He needed all the oxygen he could get.

It's late. I am sleepy. I think will go to bed and read in the morning.

June 25

I woke up and I took Zak to camp. I come home and read my bible. I prayed earlier. I am still thanking God for my husband's healing and for saving him. *(I really thought God was going to heal him.)*

I forgot in my anger I had told God that I was tired. "Do what you want to do." I know now that you don't speak anything out of your mouth when you don't know how it is going to end.

I took his vital signs. I gave him his cereal. He only ate a small amount.

Frances called for us to have prayer. She told me about last night's message that Pastor Callahan preached at Word of Faith Church. She prayed. The anointing was here. I went to the State Board of Health to apply for Otis' Birth Certificate, and I went by Dr. Luke's office to drop some papers off.

I tried to encourage Otis to get out of bed this morning. He tried to tell me it was better for him to stay in bed. He says he feels better but not strong. I told him to get up and give God something to work with. Help him defeat the devil.

I prayed with Otis, and as I was praying, it was impressed upon me to tell him to gargle. I felt that it would help his voice. He gargled, but he thought I just wanted him to refresh his breath. I told him to expect something when he gargles again.

He didn't want any lunch, so I gave him a can of pulmocare to drink. I feel he has to have some nourishment.

His cousin Pop came to see him. That got him out of bed. Pop prayed with him before he left. Otis stayed in the living room and read the newspaper.

As I was sitting in the den talking on the telephone, I looked out the window saw Deacon and Sister Givens coming. They came in and we had a beautiful fellowship. He prayed for Otis too.

It is such a blessing to have so many people praying for you. We just sat and talked about the Lord. When they left, I heard Otis praising the Lord.

Miss Sister, Mae, and I went to Ryan's as we do every Friday, most times. We had dinner, stopped by Pic and Sav, and I came home.

At home, Otis asked me to give him his leftover oxtails. I warmed them up. He only ate a small amount. He says he doesn't have an appetite.

I can hear him just lying in bed telling God thank you. I told him earlier that it was up to him and God and the devil. The devil wants to discourage him and make him give up and God wants him to live. God wants your whole heart. Earlier, Sister Givens told Otis that he was blessed to have a wife that knows the Lord and is serving Him. Otis said he was thankful for it.

As I sat at the table going through some bills, the doorbell rang. I looked out. It was Harry from next door. I knew what he was coming to tell me when I saw tears in his eyes. Herbert, his daddy, had left us today at about four or five o'clock. He just put his arms around me and cried, saying, "We just have to be strong and Herbert doesn't have to suffer anymore." I told him I would make a phone call for him.

I asked how Ruth, his mother was doing. He said she was trying to hold up. I thought back. It was a year this month that Darryl was killed. (Harry's brother) They had a memorial in the paper last week.

I tried calling our neighbor Pop to tell him, but all I got was a busy signal. I will have to remember to call in the morning. I called another neighbor, Frances. We all have been in this neighborhood a long time. Ruth and Herbert were living next door when we moved out here. Otis took it pretty good, I think. He said too that Herbert didn't have to suffer anymore.

As I sit here in the bathroom writing, at times I think I hear Otis telling the Lord thank you. Earlier, when Deacon Givens finished praying, we were all just thanking God. I felt the anointing on me and this song came to mind that says, "Is your all on the altar of sacrifice laid? Your heart, does the spirit control? You can only be blessed and have peace and sweet rest when you yield Him your body and soul." I told them that the song had come on my mind, and I told Otis it was between him and God. I feel that God wants his undivided attention as with all of us.

Those words, I want your undivided attention is what Otis said to me when we first started dating. I remember smiling until my sister said, "I wish someone made me smile like that."

I tried calling Ruth. Ashley, one of her friends, answered the phone and told me she had a lot of company, and she will tell her I called.

June 26

I slept late. I got up and prayed. I tried to call Pop again. The phone was busy. I took Otis' vital signs and gave him his breakfast. I finally got Pop on the phone and told him Harry wanted me to let him know about Herbert passing.

Otis came to the den and sat down to watch TV. I went to the bathroom. I heard the doorbell ring. I went down the hall and peaked because I still had on my PJs. It was Doc and Thelma Walker, classmates of Otis.

I went to take a bath. I got myself cleaned up and dressed. I went in the den and sat and talked with them. After they left, I fixed lunch for all of us. Otis wanted a can of beef stew. He ate that very well. Miss Sister and I had sausage.

I went into the den. Otis wanted to know what I was about to do. I told him I was about to start on the front closet. He said okay. I asked him what you want to do. He said nothing. I told him he was lying. He finally told me he wants to go to Mama's to take a watermelon.

We got in the car and went to mama's. Big Man was there. He took the melon out of the car. Mama came to the car because Otis didn't want to get out. We left and came home.

We saw Minister Jones at the 13th Street Ministry. He was cutting the hedges. We waved at him.

We were home for a little while before Big Man, Flammie, Mama and the children came. Everyone went into the den. Flammie left Rashad and went shopping. Pop and Margaret came over for a little while. Big Man and I went out east to unclog a line. He got it working. Thank God. Trey, Cyn, and Kailyn came by to see us. He and his daddy had prayer and praise. On my way home from the east side, I stopped by Mary Ann's Fried Chicken. It was good.

Goodnight.

June 27

I woke up early. I had to cook dinner before going to church. I made a peach cobbler for Mazella's district meeting. I had to go to the store to get milk. I had forgotten it.

Otis told me we had to go to church today. He had tears in his eyes. He said he was going too. He ate breakfast well and started getting ready. I got dressed too. At the car, I asked which direction to go. He said Philippian.

As we were getting ready to get in the car, this young lady came up to him, hugged him, and said, "I just couldn't stay away." I wanted to say, "Why did you have to stay away? We have been knowing each other for years." I was already suspicious of them. This made me angry. I kept my cool and got him into the car.

We got to church just before service started. We had to sit up front. It was a very unusual service. We just praised the Lord and healing took place. Pastor began calling out people and conditions. It was really anointed. Pastor went into the pulpit and came back saying the Lord said, "Pray for Wright." He laid hands on Otis. He was so weak when we left home. It took all he could muster to get dressed.

Melba Moore was in church and she was prayed for too. She also sang a song, "Blessed Assurance." God blessed.

We got home and ate dinner. Three young ladies from Bethlehem came and brought Otis a fruit dish from The Voices of Bethlehem. They are interested in finding a church, and I invited them to Philippian. They said they are coming Friday night. Otis sat and talked with them and thanked them.

Otis went to lay down. He said he couldn't get comfortable. He soon got up and went in the living room. I asked what was wrong. He said he felt as if something was missing. He felt a void. He said he wanted to be filled with the Holy Ghost. I looked for scripture to read to him. I told him to let us just praise the Lord. We did, and the anointing of the Lord was there. We even repeated the sinner's prayer again, just in case sin was there. We praised the Lord for a long time. He went back to the bedroom and got his oxygen.

I didn't think he was getting ready to meet the Lord.

Later, he told me he had a nagging pain in his back and leg, and sometimes, in his scrotum.

Sometimes, I can hear him thanking God or saying, "Lord Jesus."

I called Trey and told him his daddy wanted to be filled. He told me Otis had told him last night and that is why they had been praising. I told him how Otis said he didn't sleep last night. We decided that God was dealing with him.

I told Otis to wait on God, and when he couldn't sleep, ask God what he wanted him to do.

It is time for me to go to sleep.

June 28

I woke up when the phone rang. It was Deborah H. telling me Fred and Zak were on the way. I laid there until the doorbell rang.

I let Zak in and went back to sleep. Zak went in the den to watch TV. I woke and took him to camp. I came home and did my morning rituals.

I prayed before taking Zak to camp. Otis' vital signs were good. He says he feels weak. He talked for a long time. He told me that I had every right to have left him a long time ago, and if I did, he would have blamed me for that too. He stated, he knows now that it wasn't all my fault. He told me how he hated to come home. I told him I hated coming home too. Now, we see all the wasted time.

I am not a good housekeeper. He likes things to look nice, so I disappointed him, and he disappointed me. He tried to make things hard for me. He acknowledges saying things to hurt me.

I see what God is doing, I think. He is allowing Otis to look over his life and be able to ask for forgiveness.

He ate a Nutri-Grain and drank an Ensure Plus for breakfast, and he wanted to call the doctor about his appetite. Dr. Luke said his heart is probably not pumping the blood like it should and that's causing the tiredness. He told me a pill for him to take for appetite. We already have some of those.

He is still on me about getting everything back in place. I am doing it, but it takes time. I was able to clean the front closet and put a piece of carpet in there. Also, I was able to place a few boxes in there. Otis had to take the doors down for me.

Tony came by after work. He talked to his daddy and ministered to him. Trey came by while Tony and Otis were in the room and joined them. They had prayer and praise. Otis admitted earlier he was afraid to completely let go (away from the doctor).

Tony put the doors up to the closet for me before he left. Trey stayed and ministered some more. Brother Lauray came by asking for Trey. He wanted to come in and go back there, but I would not let him. I hope I didn't offend him.

Tricey called, and as we were talking, the doorbell rang. I told her it was probably Brother Lauray, and I will call her back. It was him. I told him I hope I didn't hurt his feelings. He told me I had. He said he just wanted to come in. He offered to cut my yard. Trey came from the back and got his keys to leave. They walked out of the door together.

Later, I fixed Otis a plate for dinner. He didn't want to eat. I told him Tricey had asked if he was eating. I called her and was talking to her while he ate. He ate all of it. I teased him, telling him he only ate because I was talking to Tricey. He just smiled.

I washed the dishes and decided to mop the kitchen floor. Just as I finished moping, my sister that lives in Fort Lauderdale, FL, called to let me know she will be coming to the family reunion.

As I sit here typing my story, I thought back to one of the times when Otis was in the hospital. I can't remember all the details as to what had him in there. This was the time that both of us talked to the doctor not knowing that both of us asked the doctor how much time Otis had left. He told both of us three to six months. We talked about it. It was at this visit that Otis told me about a television ministry for prayer. The first thing they asked for was a credit card number. He then said that my phone ministry (Philippian) prayed for him and didn't ask for anything.

He looked at me and told me he always thought Tony, our youngest son was just like me, but realize now how much he was like him.

I remember that as the nurse was wheeling him out to get in the car, I heard from God, "Last time." I got so happy. I thought that he didn't have to back in the hospital. I just knew he was healed. No more hospitals. I was looking forward to us spending time together and loving on each other. Forget what the doctor said.

After I talked with my sister, I was so tired and sleepy. I read my bible and went to bed. As I was reading, I was thinking about Otis. The thought came to my mind to ask God what can I do to help Otis? As soon as the thought entered my mind, the same answer came that came when I prayed for what to do last week. "Wait on me," the Lord said. So, I'll just have to wait on the Lord and hope He strengthens Otis' heart, body, and soul.

I can hear Otis off and on saying, "Thank you, Lord. Thank you, Jesus. Have mercy Lord." So, I'll just wait on the Lord.

July 1993

July 2

I was not sure about going to the family reunion in Valdosta, Georgia. Otis insisted that I go. I was thinking, "He is too weak," but he decided to go. I didn't want to go without him. I knew his sisters would take good care of him.

It was too late for us to get a portable oxygen tank. We had a big one that I thought would be enough.

I had to rent a car for the trip. While driving, I was directed to cut across to another highway, but the traffic was going so good that I kept going and the traffic stopped and slowed to a crawl. What usually takes two hours took about four because of the accident.

By the time Otis and I got to the house, he was tired and so was I. We got him in the house and plugged up the big oxygen tank. Everyone was glad to see him. He sat in the room with my brother-in-law, Nathaniel. Our son Trey came in the room and started singing, "His Eyes is on the Sparrow." It was so beautiful.

We were in my old room, in the house that I grew up in, in Valdosta, Georgia. My sister Bernice and her husband Nathaniel and daughter Robin live here now.

Otis was sitting in a nice chair. He seems to be okay. The children were playing and having fun. They were so glad to see each other. At the hotel, I got Otis settled in the room. My sister Deborah was in the room next door. She came up from Fort Lauderdale, FL. My sister Mary and some of her grandchildren came down from Detroit, MI.

July 3

Everyone was at the house. The kids played and had fun. The food was good. My sister Jenifer who lives in Valdosta came over to the house. We talked and caught up on everything. My sister Deborah will be going back to Fort Lauderdale. Mary and her grands are going to Orlando to have more fun. Beverly and her sons Bobby and Brooks were down from Michigan also.

The weather was bad. It was raining. Tony, Deborah, and the children were leaving. Otis told Tony not to leave. Tony was determined to go. Otis told him to leave, but leave his daughter-in-law and grandchildren. They left anyway and got home safe.

July 4

Trey and Cyn and the kids went to North Carolina to see her sister. The other family members went to the family church, Tabernacle Holiness Church.

I stayed at the hotel with Otis. He is resting in bed looking at TV.

This was the last day. I went over to Bernice's house to see everyone off. I got some food and went back to the hotel. When I got back to the hotel, Otis said he was all right. I start rubbing on his feet for no reason. They were cold. I kept moving my hand up his body. It was cold. I thought about an old saying that I heard growing up. If the body gets cold up to the heart, a person dies. I was scared. I hurried and got my sister Deborah and told her we had to leave. I packed Otis' things up, got him in the car and came back to Jacksonville.

At home, Otis sat in the chair by the door. I got Tony to go with me to take the car back.

When we got back, Otis was still sitting in the same spot. I ask him why he didn't go lay down. He said he just wanted to sit there.

Some of the people from the church came by. He sat with them in the den for a while. They talked and prayed. Then, I heard Otis praying. He told the Lord that he will do whatever he wants him to do.

Tony had come in before he left and talked to his dad.

As Otis sat with the men from the church, he started breathing funny. I asked if he wanted me to call his doctor. He said me, "No, call rescue." I called rescue.

While we were waiting, Trey and Cynthia and the kids came. Trey said the Lord told him to stop by here first. Beverly, Bobby, and Brooks stopped by also. They got to see uncle Notis, as Bobby called him, again.

Rescue came and took Otis to Saint Luke hospital. They were asking me questions about a living will. When I told them I didn't have one, he said we should get one.

I found out that the living will give instructions on whether to do resuscitation or not. At the hospital, they put me out and told me where to go. I stood at the corner of the building looking to see if Otis was still alive.

When they pulled him out, he was looking around for me. I went in the building to the ER and waited for them to call me back. Trey, Tony and Otis' brother and sister came to the hospital.

While we were in the ER, Otis asked me if I was going to be all right. I talked real brave. I told him I will be fine, but I wasn't thinking about him really dying. I told him all I wanted to know is that he knows that he knows that he was saved. He said, "I know."

Then, he was breathing funny again. He told me to get the nurse. I got the nurse and the other people start talking to me, asking if I wanted to call his pastor. They knew what was going on, but I didn't. I called his pastor and told him that we were in the ER. They worked with him and got him stable. They took Otis to a room, but not ICU as they had done the other times.

We were all around the bed and Trey was praying. All of a sudden, Otis said, "Be quiet." I went to the bed and bent down and said, "You don't want us to pray?" He said, "You can pray, but keep it down."

He started to breathe as if he couldn't get his breath. I called the nurse, she came in, but she didn't do anything.

I got closer to him, in his face. He kissed my lips, and he was gone.

I started saying, "It's not supposed to be like this." I wanted to pray. Trey said, "No momma. Let him go."

I was in denial, thinking God was going to heal him.

I later find out that Otis had told Trey he was leaving. I know now that's why they put him in a regular room instead of ICU. They knew he was at the end.

He lost the battle to cancer. His brother Pop was in the room when he died. He was so hurt he told Otis to suffer some more. It was hard on him too because he looked up to his big brother.

His pastor got there after he passed. The nurses, from ICU, heard that he had passed and the came to the floor, asking why he didn't come to them. I could not tell them anything.

His sisters and brother left and went to their mother's house.

I made the arrangements with the hospital as to what funeral home will get the body. I had them call Marion Graham Funeral Home.

Trey and I left the hospital. As we were walking out of that familiar door, I remembered that the last time he was wheeled out of the hospital, I heard, "Last time." I thought he was healed.

Trey and I went by my mother-in-law's house. Everyone was crying. Trey took me home. Tony came down. He felt bad because he left hospital thinking his dad was going to be all right as he had been all the other times.

Here I am all alone after everyone left.

I tried to call Tricey's friends in Tallahassee because I didn't want her to be alone when I tell her. I could not reach any of them. I finally called her and told her what happened. She said that she was okay.

I thought about all the years we had been together. Thirty-one years. We had just celebrated that on June 24th. I felt as if someone had taken my heart out. I told someone that I would not wish that on anyone.

Otis died on the anniversary of my mother's funeral, eight years earlier.

July 6

I had to make funeral arrangements. It didn't take long. The owner of the funeral home's son is a close friend of my daughters. They are in college FSU in Tallahassee. Mr. Graham was very helpful and courteous. There was still a lot to do. We decided to wear navy blue. We went shopping. My sister Mae and I had suits alike.

After all those years, the suit is still in my closet.

I decided to have the funeral at my church because it was larger and more accommodating. His church members did not like that at all. I had talked to my pastor about it, and he said it was okay for Otis' church to have full control. They still made a big deal out of it. Pastor Callahan would not say anything at the funeral. One of my girlfriends called to tell me, her husband, who is a police officer, will provide help for the funeral, so that is something I didn't have to pay for.

On the day of the funeral, one of Otis' classmates came to the house to be with me. At the church, I saw his coworkers, classmates, Masonic brothers and many friends. My girlfriends, Herma, Mary, and Faith were there. The service was great. The spirit of the Lord was present and that made it easier.

During the viewing, as everyone was going around, Herma came by. I got up and went to the casket and told her, "You were there in the beginning. (She introduced us.) Here you are at the end." We just embraced each other and laughed.

When it was time to close the casket, Trey, Tony, Tricey and I went to the casket to put the covering over him and closed the casket.

That was our way of saying, "Good night. Love you."

So, to my husband,
and the father of my children,
Good Night, Otis.

We Love You.

www.ingramcontent.com/pod-product-compliance
Lightning Source LLC
Chambersburg PA
CBHW071527080526
44588CB00011B/1583